making disciples of
oral learners

*To proclaim His story
where it has not been known before...*

ION / LCWE

Originally Published as
Lausanne Occasional Paper (LOP) No. 54
"Making Disciples of Oral Learners"
Issues Group No. 25

Avery Willis – Convener, Steve Evans – Co-Convener
Mark Snowden – Facilitator

Lausanne Committee for World Evangelization
2004 Forum for World Evangelization
Pattya, Thailand
September 29 to October 5, 2004

Editorial Committee:
Samuel Chiang
Steve Evans
Annette Hall
Grant Lovejoy, chair
David Payne
Sheila Ponraj
Avery Willis

The list of all Issues Group No. 25 participants and contributors to this paper appears at
the end of this edition.

Series Editor for the 2004 Forum LOPs (commencing with no. 30): David Claydon.
In encouraging the publication and study of the Occasional Papers, the Lausanne
Committee or World Evangelization does not necessarily endorse every viewpoint
expressed in these papers.

This edition published by International Orality Network
In cooperation with Elim Publishing
Lima, NY USA

To proclaim His story where it has not been known before (re: Rom. 15:20)

Photos: Langfia Ayeona, Taitiana Cardeal, Steve Evans
Book and Jacket Design: Mike Mirabella

ISBN 1-59919-018-4

Printed in USA

 # Contents

1

growing awareness of a global situation

Growing Awareness
of a Global Situation

PASTOR Dinanath of India tells his story of ministry among his people:[1]

> I was saved from a Hindu family in 1995 through a cross-cultural missionary. I had a desire to learn more about the word of God and I shared this with the missionary. The missionary sent me to Bible College in 1996. I finished my two years of theological study and came back to my village in 1998. I started sharing the good news in the way as I learnt in the Bible College. To my surprise my people were not able to understand my message. A few people accepted the Lord after much labour. I continued to preach the gospel, but there were little results. I was discouraged and confused and did not know what to do.

But then Pastor Dinanath's story takes a major turn:

> In 1999 I attended a seminar where I learnt how to communicate the gospel using different oral methods. I understood the problem in my communication as I was mostly using a lecture method with printed books,

---

1   The account from Pastor Dinanath is provided by S. D. Ponraj and Sheila Ponraj.

which I learnt in the Bible school. After the seminar I went to the village but this time I changed my way of communication. I started using a storytelling method in my native language. I used gospel songs and the traditional music of my people. This time the people in the villages began to understand the gospel in a better way. As a result of it people began to come in large numbers. Many accepted Christ and took baptism. There was one church with few baptized members in 1999 when I attended the seminar. But now in 2004, in six years we have 75 churches with 1350 baptized members and 100 more people are ready for baptism.

The account described in the first part of Pastor Dinanath's story is not an isolated instance. The gospel is being proclaimed now to more people than at any other time in history, yet many of those are not really *hearing* it. Unfortunately, most evangelical leaders do not realize the magnitude of the problem. Those affected by it include the 4 billion oral communicators of the world: people who can't, don't, or won't take in new information or communicate by literate means. Oral communicators are found in every cultural group in the world and they constitute approximately two-thirds of the world's population! Yet we are not communicating the gospel effectively with them. We will not succeed in reaching the majority of the world unless we make some crucial changes.

Ironically, an estimated 90% of the world's Christian workers presenting the gospel use highly literate communication styles. They use the printed page or expositional, analytical and logical presentations of God's word. This makes it difficult, if not impossible, for oral learners to hear and understand the message and communicate it to others. As the ones bringing the message, it is our responsibility to communicate our message in their terms. The pages that follow are intended to help point the way for us to do that.

Current estimates indicate that around two-thirds of the world's population are oral communicators either by necessity or by choice. To effectively communicate with them, we must defer to their oral communication style. Our presentations must match their oral learning styles and preferences. Instead of using outlines, lists, steps and principles we need to use culturally relevant approaches they would understand. Are we willing to seek God to become better stewards of the Great Commission and address these issues in serving Him in these last days? The Lausanne Forum of 2004 has responded to this challenge in the form of the Issue Group focused on "Making Disciples of Oral Learners."

This terminology, "making disciples" and "oral learners," is a mix of the familiar and unfamiliar. By "making disciples" we mean enabling people to respond in faith to Jesus Christ and to grow in relationship with Him and others with the goal of obeying everything that Jesus commanded (Mt. 28:20). Or as Paul described it in more detail, making disciples involves bringing people to be

> ...filled with the knowledge of [God's] will in all spiritual wisdom and understanding, so that [they] will walk in a manner worthy of the Lord, to please Him in all respects, bearing fruit in every good work and increasing in the knowledge of God; strengthened with all power, according to His glorious might, for the attaining of all steadfastness and patience; joyously giving thanks to the Father, who has qualified us to share in the inheritance of the saints in light" (Col. 1:9b-12, NASB).

Normally discipling takes place in the context of churches that make disciples and plant other churches. By "oral learners" we mean those people who learn best and whose lives are most likely to be transformed when instruction comes in oral forms. Many groups transmit their beliefs, heritage, values and other important information by means of stories, proverbs, poetry, chants, music, dances, ceremonies and rites of passage. The spoken, sung, or chanted word associated with these activities often consists of ornate and elaborate ways to communicate. Those who use these art forms well are highly regarded among their people. Cultures which use these forms of communication are sometimes called "oral cultures."

The members of these societies are referred to as "oral learners" or "oral communicators." In this discussion, we use the terms "oral learner" and "oral communicator" interchangeably at times. With the phrase oral "learner" the focus is more on the receiving act—hearing an oral communication. With the phrase oral "communicator" the focus is more on the act of telling. These societies are relational, group-oriented, face-to-face cultures. Most of the members of these societies learn best through aural means.

Those who have grown up in highly literate societies tend to think of literacy as the norm and oral communication as a deviation. That is not so. All societies, including those having a highly literate segment, have oral communication at their core. Oral communication is the basic function on which writing and literacy is based. When literacy persists in a culture for generations, it begins to change the way people think, act and communicate—so much so that the members of that literate society may not even realize how their communication styles are different from those of the majority of the world who are oral communicators. These members of a literate society then tend to communicate the gospel in the literate style that speaks to them.

But oral learners find it difficult to follow literate-styled presentations, even if they are made orally. It is not enough to take materials created for literates and simply read them onto a recorded format. Making something audible does not necessarily make it an "oral" style of communication. Not everything on a CD or audiotape is "oral." Some of it is clearly literate in its style even though it is spoken or audible. The same thing is true of other media products created for literate audiences. They may have literate stylistic features that confuse oral learners.

Some people are oral learners because of their limited education. They may not read or write at all, or they may read with difficulty. Many oral learners can read but prefer learning by oral means. If their culture is traditionally oral, they frequently prefer to learn through oral methods even if they are highly educated. When many people in a culture are oral learners, it affects the whole culture and permeates many aspects of people's lives, such as thought processes and decision-making. Scholars call this whole cluster of characteristics and effects "orality." The Deaf community displays many of these traits that scholars associate with the term orality, though the Deaf cannot properly be called "oral."[2] Likewise, there are literates who demonstrate many characteristics associated with the concept of orality, an effect referred to as "secondary orality." (*Secondary orality* will be addressed in detail in chapter six.)

In summary, approximately two-thirds of the world's population lives by orality. Many of them have no other choice because they have inadequate literacy skills, but others who are quite literate strongly prefer to learn via oral means. Together they comprise an oral majority who cannot or will not learn well through print-based instruction. This poses a challenge to those who want to communicate effectively with them.

After listening to a speaker discuss the challenge that orality poses, a ministry leader approached the speaker. "If what you say is true," he told the speaker, "we will have to rethink everything we are doing." He was right. Taking orality seriously can revolutionize ministries—and has the potential to greatly increase our effectiveness. But what should we do differently? The following chapters describe specific ways to improve effectiveness in making disciples of oral learners. They describe practical steps that various churches, organizations and agencies are taking. A number of them share a common vision that addresses the predominance of oral communicators in the world. That common vision is:

---

2   Deaf with an upper case "D" by common practice refers to the people group or population segment, in contrast to lower case "deaf" referring to the physical characteristic.

• God's word for every "tribe, tongue, people and nation";

• addressing the issue of orality;

• resulting in church planting movements;

• providing resources for oral, chronological, narrative presentations of God's word, in order to disciple and equip leaders.

To these issues we now turn.

2
▽

God's Word
for the
whole

world

God's Word
for the Whole World

▽

WHAT is the hope of reaching the four billion persons who are oral learners? What is the hope for getting God's word to the speakers of the four thousand languages still without His word?[3]

The answer comes from Jesus' own model: "...with many similar parables Jesus spoke the word to them, *as much as they could understand*" (Mk. 4:33 NIV, emphasis added). In fact, the passage goes on to say: "He did not say anything to them without using a parable" (Mk. 4:34a NIV). Jesus chose his teaching style to match his listeners' capacities. So should we. Jesus used familiar oral means that they understood. So can we.

One straightforward way to communicate to oral learners in a way they will understand is for them to hear the stories of the Bible in an oral, sequential pattern that they can absorb and remember. The communication of stories in this way has come to be referred to as "chronological Bible storying." It is a proclamation of God's word in a culturally relevant way that oral learners can understand and respond to.

---

3   Statistics as of Sep. 30, 2004 from Wycliffe International indicate 4558 languages without any of the Bible, out of the 6913 languages currently spoken in the world (see *Ethnologue*, 15th ed.). Dec. 31, 2003 statistics from the United Bible Societies indicate only 2355 languages have some or all of the Bible. Of these, only 414 have an adequate Bible, 1068 have an adequate New Testament, and 873 have at least one book of the Bible (see http://www.biblesociety.org/latestnews/latest273-slr2003stats.html).

A "storying" approach to ministry involves selecting and crafting stories that convey the essential biblical message, in a way that is sensitive to the worldview of the receptor society. The stories are faithful to the biblical text, and at the same time told in a natural, compelling manner in the heart language. They are expressed in the manner in which that society conveys a treasured, true story. The process also is done in a way that facilitates the hearers in processing the story in a culturally relevant way—normally involving some sort of discussion about or interaction with the story.

Without the presence of God's word there will be no true spiritual movements. Without God's word, an incipient movement will ultimately collapse, splinter, fall prey to cults, or face syncretism with existing local beliefs and practices. Unbelievers need Christians to provide His word in culturally appropriate formats in order for them to understand it and respond to it, but understanding and responding is still not enough for a spiritual movement. Those who respond need to be able to reproduce it—to share it themselves with others who can, in turn, share it with others, with this pattern being repeated many times over. A spiritual movement of this sort can provide a foundation for faith, witness, and church life. For this to happen in an oral society and involve the majority of those oral communicators who will likely remain oral communicators for their lifetime, the process will have to be an oral one for evangelism, discipleship, leader training and church planting. Because of the communication and learning styles of oral communicators, reflecting their thought and decision-making processes, this should be primarily through narrative presentations of God's word.

This does not mean that we discourage literacy or neglect literates. Experience shows that once oral learners accept the gospel, some will have the desire and persistence to become literate in order to read the Bible for themselves. The development of oral strategies is not a deterrent to translating the Bible into every language. In fact, the opposite is true. These burgeoning church planting movements that result from an oral proclamation will need the whole counsel of God. Requiring

11

non-Christians to learn to read just so that they can consider the Christian faith puts unnecessary obstacles in their path.

We wish all peoples had the written translation of the Scripture in their heart language. But, for the illiterate, written Scripture is not accessible even if it is available in their own language. On the other hand, a Bible translation program that begins with the oral presentation of the Bible through storying and continues with a translation and literacy program is the most comprehensive strategy for communicating the word of God in their heart language. It offers a viable possibility of making disciples of oral learners while at the same time providing the whole counsel of God.

We do not want our call for oral approaches to be seen as setting oral and literate approaches in opposition to one another. It is not a matter of "either-or," but "both-and." Again, the Bible itself gives the model. There are examples throughout the Scriptures where both the written word of God and the spoken word of God are given prominence, often side by side. For example, Moses wrote down the words of the Law (Deut. 31-33). God instructed him to write the words down in a song. God also instructed him to teach the song to the Israelites so that they would always have it in their hearts and on their lips and always remember it.

Similarly in today's world, we envision a systemic approach to evangelism, discipleship, church planting and leadership development that can involve oral, audio, audio-visual media and print. A systemic, sequential approach with a society of largely oral communicators, for example, might begin with oral Bible storying. It could then possibly begin to involve audio and radio presentations of these same oral stories and other audio and radio products of a broader array based on translated biblical material.[4] In some cases primary visual products may be produced and effectively used.[5] Then the process in some

---

4   Examples of some of these sorts of audio and radio presentations in vernacular languages include Global Recordings Network's various Scripture resources; the *JESUS Film* audio versions; *Lives of the Prophets, Life of Jesus* and *Lives of the Apostles* audio versions; Faith Comes by Hearing dramatized recordings of the New Testament; and the Radio Bible, which consists of 365 fifteen-minute broadcasts of stories from the Old and New Testaments. These are described in the Resources section.

5   Examples of primary visual products can include print illustrations and booklets

situations may move on to the preparation and distribution of audio-visual products based on translation of further biblical material.[6] Throughout the approach the undergirding process of Bible translation, at first orally and then in a literate manner, provides the entire counsel of God.

In a sequential approach like this, the first biblical stories we use focus very intently on the unique cultural perspective of the people. Specificity to that culture is crucial in order for them to understand the gospel well and embrace Christ. The same will be true of the stories we use in initial discipleship. Later stages in the strategy will give them ever-larger portions of the Bible; at that point our focus will have shifted from cultural specificity to providing complete books of the Bible, a New Testament and finally the whole Bible.

God's word has transforming impact on people's lives when we present it in ways that they can understand it. For example, missionaries worked for twenty-five years with the Tiv tribe in central Nigeria and saw only twenty-five baptized believers as a result.[7] That is an average of one believer per year of ministry. Their medium of communication was preaching, which they had learned in Bible school was the proper way to evangelize.

Then some young Tiv Christians set the gospel story to musical chants, the indigenous medium of communication. Almost immediately the gospel began to spread like wildfire and soon a quarter million Tivs were worshipping Jesus. The Tivs were not as resistant as the missionaries had thought. A

---

depicting scenes from Bible stories and products like Deaf Missions visual recordings.

6   Examples of audio-visual products are the *JESUS Film* and related Genesis and Luke videos; *God's Story;* and *The Hope.*

7   This story is taken from C. Peter Wagner, *Strategies for Church Growth* (Ventura, California: Regal Books, 1987), 91-92.

change in method brought abundant fruit. Prior to this the gospel had been "proclaimed," but it had not been heard! The communication strategy chosen had not spoken to the heart of the people. This story underscores that groups may not be necessarily unresponsive, but have not yet received the gospel in their learning style. Where traditional literate methods have failed to reach people, appropriate oral strategies have succeeded.

When Christian workers follow these principles, non-Christians are more likely to give the gospel a hearing, more likely to respond in faith to it, and more likely to spread it enthusiastically to their friends, relatives and neighbours. In the Togolese town of Kpele-Dafo, for instance, the hamlet sprang to life when the message came: "The storyteller is coming!"[8] The sound of drumming announced the coming of the storyteller. Men left their game of *adí,* tailors closed shop, and yawning children roused themselves. The drumming intensified as the storyteller took his place in the center of the village, where he seated himself on a low, carved bench. The elders of the village arrived in their finery and the animated storyteller, Antoine, exchanged ritual, formalized greetings with his audience. The fetish priestess, clothed in white and wearing her horsehair amulet, stood near, watching intensely.

As night fell and the logs crackled in the fire, Antoine began in melodic, poetic style: *"In the beginning, God created the heavens and the earth..."* When he reached the repeated phrase, *"And God saw that it was good,"* he sang a song composed in their familiar call and response style. He sang a line about God's creative work and the villagers sang back, *"And God saw that it was good."* The villagers quickly memorized their part and sang

---

8   This story is from Carla Bowman, *Communications Bridges to Oral Cultures* (Tucson AZ, Scriptures In Use, 2004).

it enthusiastically. Before long, the villagers began dancing too, to express their delight at this God who created a good world. The village headman joined in the dance, signaling his approval of the story and the event. Antoine continued his story long into the night, accompanied by the sound of drumming and joined in his song by the villagers. When the fire had burned low and the story-song finally ended, no one wanted to leave. The whole experience had engulfed them. A new truth was dawning and their world would never be the same.

Antoine returned many times over the next several weeks, bringing story after story in this way—stories about Abraham and his sons, about the other prophets, about Jesus and God's community. These stories spoke to the villagers' longings, needs and practices, prompting long conversations with Antoine and among themselves. Gently but firmly the Holy Spirit used the stories to do his transforming work. In time extended families made God's story their own story, the God of the Bible their God. A fetish priest burned his amulets, talismans and jujus because he no longer needed their protection.

The same storytelling approach was used to bring about the surrender of strongholds and for discipleship. Through Bible storytelling the word of God came to life in the African context. The biblical stories continued as the people of Kpele-Dafo grew in their newfound faith, meeting in house churches and taking this message to neighboring villages. The same process has now taken place throughout the Volta region of Togo, Benin, and Ghana, resulting in a movement of people to Christ.

Five key principles were at work at Kpele-Dafo.
- The word of God is more effectively communicated through appropriate cultural relationships.
- The word of God will be best heard and understood when we use appropriate oral strategies.
- The word of God is most effectively proclaimed when worldview issues of the unreached are addressed; stories and other cultural forms do this more effectively by inviting listeners to identify with the message.

- The word of God changes individuals, cultures, and worldviews.
- The word of God can be passed along by ordinary Christians if they receive it in appropriate oral forms.

In both these cases the use of familiar, accepted forms of communicating helped to make the biblical message less foreign. People could easily participate in the event. The word became readily available to them. They entered into the stories and the stories entered into them.

In many parts of the unreached world, there is open hostility to evangelistic activity. Crusades, mass evangelism and public preaching are not welcome. Bible studies and open witnessing draw negative responses. In these situations storying can be more fully appreciated. Storying is not confrontational. It is not preaching. It is not overt teaching. It is merely conveying the stories of God's Word, dialoguing about them and leaving the results to God! Most of the time the hearers do not even realize that their values are changing until they can no longer deny the truth. His word says that it will not return void or empty. So, the power of His word, combined with the power of the Holy Spirit, does amazing things! These stories can go where the printed Bible sometimes cannot go. They can cross borders, enter jail cells, even go into the heart of Muslim, Hindu, animist or socialist homes! They can penetrate the heart of the one listening and change that person's life for eternity.

3

oral
communicators
and
oral
cultures ▷

Oral Communicators
and Oral Cultures

DEVELOPING proficiency in using oral strategies involves several tasks. Literates who want to communicate effectively in oral cultures need to learn about the issue of orality. Walter Ong's book, *Orality and Literacy* (1982) is a respected academic work on the topic. He offers lengthy, technical discussions of the nature of orality and the impact that the development of writing, then typography, had on oral communication and oral cultures. His approach is largely historical.

Another approach to understanding the extent and influence of orality is to consider it in relationship to literacy skills. The reality of low literacy skills even in developed countries has become apparent from a series of surveys, beginning with the National Adult Literacy Survey (NALS) administered by the U. S. Department of Education in the early 1990s.[9] Researchers found that 48 to 51% of adults in the United States scored at the two lowest levels (out of five levels) of measurable proficiency at a range of literacy skills. While results of the NALS study showed that only 4 to 6% of U. S. adults were totally illiterate, 46 to 53%

---

9   Irwin S. Kirsch, Ann Jungeblut, Lynn Jenkins and Andrew Kolstad. *A First Look at the Findings of the National Adult Literacy Survey*, 3d ed. (Washington: U. S. Department of Education, Office of Educational Research and Improvement, 2002).

were identified as unable to function adequately in a highly literate society or process lengthy written information adequately.

It was reported that while many adults at Level 1 (21-23%) could perform tasks involving simple texts and documents, all adults scoring at that level displayed difficulty using certain reading, writing and computational skills considered necessary for functioning in everyday life. Those at Level 2 could perform simple analysis, but were unable to integrate information from longer texts or documents or carry out mathematical skills when necessary information was contained in the directions. (Interestingly enough, a majority of those at Level 1 and almost all of those at Level 2 described themselves as being able to read English "well" or "very well"!).

When the International Adult Literacy Survey (IALS) tested adults in twenty-two countries from 1994-98, similar results emerged in Australia, Canada, Germany, Ireland, the U. K. and elsewhere among developed nations.[10] Although the various governments previously had claimed national literacy rates of 90% or more, the surveys revealed that many people actually had a quite limited range of literacy skills. Such people live day to day largely by oral means even if they are able to read simple, brief materials.

The Bible is certainly not simple, brief material. If half of the population in developed nations, with longstanding literate traditions, is unable to integrate information from a text like the Bible, what is the situation of those in oral cultures with no such tradition, when it comes to gaining spiritual truth?

The survey results from NALS and IALS suggest that there is not a simple, black-and-white dichotomy between "literates" and "illiterates." Other studies similarly give more revealing definitions of literacy that characterize it in terms of the different ways people function with literacy in society. One UNESCO document, for example, says:

---

10 See http://www.nifl.gov/nifl/facts/IALS.html. See also Albert Tuijnman, *Benchmarking Adult Literacy in America: An International Comparative Study* (Washington, DC: U. S. Department of Education, 2000); also available at http://www.nald.ca/fulltext/Benchmrk/2.htm. This testing has now been conducted in approximately 30 countries, with similar results.

A person is functionally literate who can engage in all those activities in which literacy is required for effective function of his or her group and community and also for enabling him or her to continue to use reading, writing and calculation for his or her own and the community's development.[11]

It is helpful for literate cross-cultural Christian workers to be aware of different degrees of literacy if they are to communicate with people in appropriate ways. These degrees of literacy reflect a continuum. One categorization of salient points along this continuum is that of James B. Slack, which describes five levels of literacy to be considered in presenting the gospel:

- "Illiterates" cannot read or write. They have never "seen" a word. In fact, the word for illiteracy in the Indonesia language is *buta huruf*, meaning "blind to letters." For oral communicators, words do not exist as letters, but as sounds related to images of events and to situations that they are seeing or experiencing.

- "Functional illiterates" have been to school but do not continue to read and write regularly after dropping out of school. Within two years, even those who have gone to school for eight years often can read only simple sentences and can no longer receive, recall or reproduce concepts, ideas, precepts, and principles through literate means. They prefer to get their information orally. Their *functional* level of illiteracy (as opposed to published data) determines how they learn, how they develop their values and beliefs, and how they pass along their culture, including their religious beliefs and practices.

- "Semi-literates" function in a gray transitional area between oral communication and literacy. Even though these individuals have normally gone to school up to 10 years and are classified in every country of the world as literates, they learn primarily by means of narrative presentations.

---

11   http://www.uis.unesco.org/ev.php?ID=5014_201&ID2=DO_TOPIC

- "Literate" learners understand and handle information such as ideas, precepts, concepts, and principles by literate means. They tend to rely on printed material as an aid to recall.

- "Highly literate" learners usually have attended college and are often professionals in the liberal arts fields. They are thoroughly print-culture individuals.[12]

Trying to reach the first three categories using customary means presents two major problems: Almost all missionaries and other Christian workers are literate or highly literate, and they communicate primarily by literate means. So they use the method they have mastered to try to communicate with oral learners who do not "hear" them. They think that if they can just simplify their outlines and exposition oral learners can grasp what they are saying. When missionaries try to reach illiterates, they believe that one of their primary tasks is to train a corps of literate nationals (who then face the same problems communicating). For these reasons it is essential that literate church leaders seek to understand orality as the first step in ministering effectively in oral cultures.

Although UNESCO reported in 2003 that almost 80% of adults worldwide can read, that statement is open to challenge. It depends on literacy statistics provided by each member nation of the United Nations. Furthermore, it allows every country's

---

12   James B. Slack, "Chronological Bible Storying" unpublished document available at http://www.chronologicalbiblestorying.com/manuals.

government to decide for itself how to determine who is literate. Malaysia, for instance, counts anyone age 10 or over who has ever enrolled in school as being literate. Other countries simply ask people if they are literate; many people say that they are, even though their reading skills may be too limited to handle text from the Bible. Many people who can write their name and read a simple sentence qualify as literate for census purposes, but they cannot read unfamiliar or lengthy materials with understanding. Their values are not changed by what they read.

In assessing the orality of a people group, it is important to keep in mind that literacy rates often vary greatly from one group to another within a single nation. Minority language groups, many of whom are unreached peoples, are less likely to be literate. Many of them have little interest in becoming literate. Those who intend to work with unreached people groups would be wise to be skeptical of governmental literacy statistics when it comes to functional literacy.

Missions groups such as the International Mission Board (Southern Baptist Convention), Scriptures In Use and others have developed materials on understanding orality and oral cultures. A selection of these is available at www.chronologicalbiblestorying.com. The annotated bibliography included with this document also suggests a wide array of resources for learning more about orality.

After developing a basic understanding of orality, literate missionaries and ministers then need to learn effective oral communication styles which are culturally relevant. In general, there is a cluster of features that oral learners have in common in processing information. They most readily process information that is concrete and sequential, and which is presented in a highly relational context. Other aspects of an effective communication style for a particular oral culture may be discovered by careful observation and participation in the life of the community.

Using culturally appropriate oral forms improves the impact of the message. Oral learners "enter" the story and as they absorb sensory data they live the story in the present tense—seeing, hearing, tasting, smelling and feeling what the persons in the story are experiencing. They hang reality on these sensory experiences.

This happened when "Fatima," an immigrant who had never been to school, attended a class to learn French.[13] As a part of the French class, she heard the story of Abraham, Sarah, and Hagar. At the end of the story Fatima said, "That's a true story."

The teacher asked, "What do you mean?"

Fatima replied, "God made Abraham a promise and Abraham didn't have the faith to wait for God. He acted on his own. And look at all the trouble that came to that family. It happens all the time. People don't have the faith to wait for God. They act on their own and they get into trouble just like Abraham did. It's a true story."

Fatima vicariously lived the story. Without prompting from the teacher, she melded the story's experiences with her experiences. The right cultural form enabled the truth to flow unimpeded into her life.

Having identified the communication forms that the culture uses, it is then crucial that ministries use the existing oral communication forms that the culture already uses (i.e.: story, music, drama, poetry, dance, proverbs, etc.) There are many examples of the impact of Bible stories when time and freedom of expression are both given in order to develop a culturally sensitive storying strategy.

One such example of the effectiveness and reproducibility of using music in orality and storying strategies comes from southeastern Africa:

> The ladies gathered on the lawn for their weekly sewing session. They were in a mountain village about forty kilometres from the shores of Lake Malawi. Usually, as the ladies sewed, they sang. I was visiting the house next door as the ladies began to sing. Because I like music, I enjoyed listening to their singing as I talked

---

13   This account is from Annette Hall. When a name is introduced within quote marks, this is an indication that this is a pseudonym. In this and some other subsequent instances, names of local workers and in some cases the people group names in the stories and case studies of this paper are not actual names. The names are changed in order to protect the security of these workers. The events told in the stories and case studies are actual events recounted or confirmed by the participants in the 2004 Lausanne Forum Issue Group on "Making Disciples of Oral Learners."

with my friends. After a while I heard a tune that was vaguely familiar, but I couldn't place it. I listened harder, concentrating on the music rather than my hosts. Then it hit me! The words and tune I was hearing were the same ones I had heard at a Yao music workshop two weeks before and forty kilometres away! In one day, the group developed fourteen Scripture songs focused on essential stories of God's word. In two weeks the song had travelled across the lake and up the mountain to a village forty kilometres away from where the workshop was held! In their own language they were singing:

"In the beginning God created, and it was good!

It was good!

In the beginning God created, and it was good!

It was good!

It was good!

It was good!

It was good!

In the beginning God created, and it was good!"

The song went on to tell about God creating the world, then man. "He made you, He made me," they sang. Finally the song ended:

"It was good!

It was good!

It was good!

It was good!

All that he had made—yes, it was good!" [14]

An example of how members of an oral culture naturally relate to oral forms of Scripture as their own comes from an experience of Herbert Klem, doing an academic research project involving various test groups:

---

14   This account is from Steve Evans.

One evening I came to a study which was crowded out with visitors. I could tell many of the visitors were Muslim elders from the very community where I was told so often that people felt too old to become Christians. I did not want all those visitors spoiling the structure of my test group, so I politely asked the visitors to leave these Christian test lessons. The wise old elder had a twinkle in his eye as he gently and politely suggested that they were having a wonderful time hearing God speak to them, and that perhaps I should be the one to leave. I did not know what to do. I was thrilled to have a Muslim man in a Bible study, and he was an elder leader, but I did not want to spoil the structure of my test. When I asked him politely to leave a second time, he grinned and challenged me to a true test of ownership of the singing Bible tapes. The one who could sing the least of the tape from memory would leave, and the one who could sing the most could stay. That was the indigenous method of proving cultural ownership.

Because of the tonal intricacies of singing oral art in that language, he knew he had me beat cold — no contest! The group cheered and proclaimed him the owner of the tape. He boasted that only a wise Yoruba man could compose and sing this kind of poetry; insiders loved it and outsiders could admire from a small distance.

The elder had been warmly attracted to the text because it had been identified with his culture, employing art forms that marked it as his cultural property, even though it was played on a tape recorder supplied by a meddling foreigner. He was pleased with the form of the message, but he was also bonding with God's Word from the book of Hebrews. He was no longer telling me this was "foreign religion" but was defending his right to hear the Scripture. Best of all, the whole group loved the entire event. [15]

---

15   Herbert Klem, "Dependence on Literacy Strategy: Taking a Hard Second

In addition to the choice of communication form, the choice of what language to use is crucial. The most effective ministry strategies among oral cultures occur when the communication is done in the heart language, the mother tongue. It is often easy to overlook the fact that people speaking over 4,000 different languages are still awaiting God's word in their heart language. Many of these groups have a long history of being a minority people in their own country. When the Bible has come to them in the past, it has often been in a printed form that they cannot read or in a language which does not speak to their heart. In fact, it might be in the language of the very people who they feel have oppressed them for many years.

However, when they hear the stories from God's word in their own language, they are often amazed and have an immediate heart response and cultural identification with that message. They may respond that indeed God has remembered them and He is for them! When they hear the message in their heart language, the words speak to them in an indescribable way. Because it is their own language, it captivates them and they want to hear more.

Stories heard in the mother tongue are easily memorized and retold to others. Oral learners can often recite large portions of scripture when they hear these passages in their mother tongue and packaged in the stories that they can easily learn and reproduce.

Effective ministries among oral cultures should be worldview sensitive in order to build bridges of understanding and confront barriers to the gospel message. Because stories possess the power to actually change how people think, feel, and behave, and to change the way they see the world, it is important to have a sequential, step-by-step process that leads them to a new, biblical worldview. What is effective in such situations is the oral communication of a set of chronological Bible stories that involve points of similarity between a culture's worldview and a biblical worldview. This incorporates "bridges" from its worldview to the biblical story. It simultaneously confronts "barriers" to the gospel, those elements of the worldview that hinder understanding and acceptance. Over

Look," *International Journal of Frontier Missions* 12:2 (April-June, 1995) 63-64.

time, confronting worldview barriers with stories of the Bible can lead them to accept a more compelling story than the stories associated with their own worldview.

An example of this account comes from the Asheninka people group in Peru:

> Alejandro, the leader, is doing great in chronological Bible storying and the people understand. He told the story of Jesus calming the waters during the storm and Cladis softly told me that she used to believe that the Owner of the Winds could be stopped by placing your axe in the ground with the blade cutting the wind, but now she knows it is God that created the winds and He is God. Also, she told me that she is not scared of the rainbows anymore because they do not kill you when you walk under them. God created the rainbow to make a promise with us. Alejandro himself came to the understanding that he can baptize the people and the people understand that they can be baptized after simply believing. So, Alejandro baptized twelve believers last week. It was a week of fiestas. Trip after trip Alejandro tells the stories, *then*, it hits them. It is such an awesome thing to be part of.[16]

Choosing stories that address worldview bridges and barriers of a specific people group or segment of society improves the likelihood that their worldview will be brought into conformity with the biblical pattern, the kingdom of God.

Understanding orality and oral cultures gives us the basis for adopting effective oral communications strategies. These understandings enable us to realize the importance of the word being shared in the mother tongue and in ways that enable the people to embrace the message from God.

---

16   This account comes from Pam Ammons, and can be found, along with other examples at: http://www.chronologicalbiblestorying.com/news/newsletters_index.htm.

4

disciples
to the core

Disciples to the Core

SYNCRETISM is "the mixing of Christian assumptions with those worldview assumptions that are incompatible with Christianity so that the result is not biblical Christianity."[17] Syncretism weakens the church, warps non-Christians' understanding of Christianity and withholds from God the full devotion and complete obedience that is rightly due to Him. So the spiritual health and vibrancy of Christian churches depends on developing a faith that is as free from syncretism as possible, a faith that is both biblical and culturally relevant. Several key elements can contribute to discipling oral learners with a minimal amount of syncretism.

The first key element in avoiding syncretism is communicating with people in their mother tongue — the language in which they learned their religion, values and cultural identity. They house their innermost thoughts in their mother tongue, so it is the language through which their worldview is most likely to change. They can explain their new faith more readily to others in their people group when they use the mother tongue. In using the

---

17   Charles Kraft, "Culture, Worldview and Contextualization," in *Perspectives on the World Christian Movement*, 3d ed., ed. Ralph D. Winter and Steven C. Hawthorne (Pasadena, CA: William Carey Library, 1999), 390.

mother tongue, one must carefully consider the key biblical terms to use in a language if there is not yet a Bible translation. Concepts like love, grace and sin, or even the basic notion like the name used for God, the Holy Spirit, or Christ need to be carefully identified. Inadequacies in this area readily lead to syncretism.

When pastors are asked why they preach in a national language or trade language instead of the local language of their congregation, they often respond that they did their theological training in the trade language and that the local language is not rich in theological terms. If the pastor does not know how to express theological terms in the local language, you can be sure that his people are not grasping these important concepts. When the pastor does not preach and teach in the local language, he is leaving the important task of choosing the correct term to interpreters who do not have the benefit of the pastor's theological training. The use of interpreters who are not trained in biblical language can result in wrong words being used for important Christian concepts and this can lead to syncretism or even heresy.

The Puinave people of Colombia were "re-discipled" when missionaries uncovered syncretism.[18] Although the Puinave had become culturally "Christian" in the 1950s, they mixed magic with their understanding of Christianity's behavioral norms. Many misunderstandings resulted from using the national language, Spanish, in their Christian activity. When New Tribes Mission workers spent seven years learning the Puinave language in the 1970s, they were surprised at the syncretistic beliefs held. At first, they tried teaching the Bible using traditional teaching methods. The Puinave nodded their agreement, but missed many of the key points.

It was only through a chronological presentation of God's word, beginning with the Old Testament and on to the Gospels, story by story, that they were able to vividly portray the holy nature and character of God, the sinful condition of man, the grip that Satan has on this world and the redeeming solution to man's predicament found in Jesus Christ. Reflecting on this

---

18   New Tribes Mission, *Now We See Clearly*, video, 1998.

redemptive panorama of God's provision, the village elder held up his thumb near to his forefinger and observed: "I came just this close from going to hell..."

Consider the example of Jesus. He taught using the common heart language of the people, rather than the trade language. Jesus spoke in the format that the common people understood such as stories, parables and proverbs. The people who heard were able to understand and apply them, bringing about transformed lives. By communicating in the heart language and using the methods that are common in the culture, we can minimize the danger of syncretism and heresy.

A second key element in reducing syncretism is to develop discipling resources that are worldview specific. Generic discipleship materials are insufficient. Certainly there are biblical essentials that every new Christian needs to know, such as prayer, worship, witness, fellowship and ministry. These practices, however, should fit the local culture under the leadership of the Holy Spirit rather than the practices of the host culture of the missionary. Kraft points out that syncretism occurs when the evangelizers impose their cultural values on the new Christians and fail to separate the evangelizers' own culture adequately from the biblical message.[19] If a certain set of discipleship materials worked well with a people group or segment of society, it is because the materials were meaningful to that worldview. The fact that they served so well among one people should serve as a caution that they will not likely meet needs as effectively in a different cultural setting.

The best discipling resource among oral communicators is not a printed booklet but an obedient Christian. Oral communicators learn by observing. Discipleship involves the disciple spending time with the more mature believer learning by following his or her example. The teaching is conducted more by watching and doing rather than just learning facts. Discipling oral learners would best follow the biblical models such as Elijah, Jesus, and Paul. For example, Paul tells the

---

19   Charles Kraft, "Culture, Worldview and Contextualization," 390.

Philippian believers, *"Whatever you have learned or received or heard from me, or seen in me–put it into practice"* (Phil. 4:9 NIV). The goal would be that the disciple would immediately become a discipler. As Paul told Timothy, *". . . the things you have heard me say in the presence of many witnesses entrust to reliable men who will also be qualified to teach others"* (2 Tim. 2:2 NIV).

A third key element in discipling oral learners in order to limit syncretism is to recognize the importance of stories in transforming a person's worldview. N. T. Wright says that stories constitute the core of every culture's worldview. (See the diagram below.) A culture houses its central convictions in its fundamental narrative, whether its narrative is implicit or explicit. The ancient mythologies that we find in cultures around the world are explicit examples of this. Those stories answer four fundamental worldview questions: Who am I? Where am I? What has gone wrong? What can be done about it? Every culture uses stories to tell us what it means to be human, what kind of world we live in, why there is suffering and pain, and what, if anything, we can do to deal with that suffering and pain. Christianity has its own distinctive answers to those worldview questions. In order to influence the worldviews of disciples, we need to tell biblical stories that offer alternative answers to the fundamental worldview questions. The Bible answers these questions with special vividness and power in the opening chapters of Genesis.[20] That is one reason it is so important to include Old Testament stories in discipling. Furthermore, when we tell biblical stories chronologically, we

---

20   What God has done to deal with the problem of sin is revealed much more fully in the Gospels and Epistles, of course, but there are references to God's redemptive plan in the early stories in Genesis.

are offering a powerful alternative worldview from the very beginning of our presentation. Biblical stories, and the view of the world embedded in them, can replace or refine the cultural stories and the worldview embedded in them.

Wright argues that this is why Jesus so often told stories, particularly parables. Jesus intended them to challenge the existing Jewish worldview and to provide an alternative picture of reality that Jesus called "the kingdom of God" or "kingdom of heaven." Wright says, "Stories are, actually, peculiarly good at modifying or subverting other stories and their worldviews. Where head-on attack would certainly fail, the parable hides the wisdom of the serpent behind the innocence of the dove, gaining entrance and favour which can then be used to change assumptions which the hearer would otherwise keep hidden away for safety."[21]

There are four areas that affect people...

The Transforming Power Of Stories!

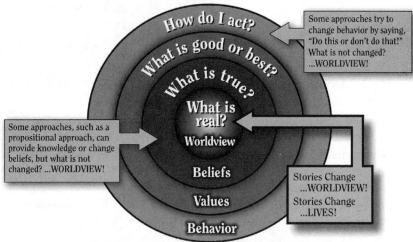

How do I act?

What is good or best?

What is true?

What is real?

Worldview

Beliefs

Values

Behavior

Some approaches try to change behavior by saying, "Do this or don't do that!" What is not changed? ...WORLDVIEW!

Some approaches, such as a propositional approach, can provide knowledge or change beliefs, but what is not changed? ...WORLDVIEW!

Stories Change ...WORLDVIEW!
Stories Change ...LIVES!

Wright says stories come into conflict with each other because worldviews and the stories which characterize them

---

21   N. T. Wright, *The New Testament and the People of God*, (Minneapolis: Fortress Press, 1992), 40.

represent the realities of one's life. People are threatened by the intrusion of an opposing worldview or story because it challenges their understanding of reality. Wright says *"The only way of handling the clash between two stories is to tell yet another story explaining how the evidence for the challenging story is in fact deceptive."*[22]

If stories anchor people's existing perspective on the world, then the best thing Christians can do in order to displace that perspective is to tell better stories, and we have them! Our stories must provide biblical answers to the essential questions of life.[23] The more biblical stories people know and can fit into a single comprehensive story of God's saving work, the more completely they are able to embrace a biblical worldview. By changing their fundamental view of the world, we hope to influence a wide array of beliefs and practices which grow out of that fundamental core.

Wright argues that stories lie at the core of a worldview; formal belief statements, including propositional and theological statements, grow out of those stories. Thus discipleship that offers only propositional teaching does not reach to the centre of the worldview. If we give only propositional teaching and do not present biblical *stories* to challenge existing worldview *stories*, we run the risk of syncretism. The cultural stories will continue to comprise the heart of the worldview and discipleship will deal only with the dimensions of the person's life represented in the outer circles in the diagram. Because propositional beliefs are generated by and reflected in the core stories, those cultural stories will continually be challenging the Christian propositional content. We wind up with the tragedy of professing Christians who assent to biblical propositions, but whose essential worldview and value system is deeply tied to worldview stories that have gone unchallenged. That mix of contradictory religious beliefs and practices is the essence of syncretism. It constitutes a failure in discipling.

A careful study of an unreached people group's worldview will reveal common ground, bridges between their worldview and

---

22   Wright, 42.
23   Wright, 38-40.

the Bible. On these matters the discipler may simply *reinforce* existing beliefs and practices. Worldview study also will disclose matters on which the people group's worldview is contrary to the biblical ideal; these contrary matters are barriers.[24] In those instances, the discipler guides converts to *replace* the existing belief or practice with the biblical one. In addition, the study may reveal issues in which the existing practices and beliefs can be *revised* into the way of Christ. This approach to discipling aims to minimize the syncretism that comes when people just adopt Christian rituals or practices, but keep intact the mythology that underlies the traditional religion. When their core stories are not challenged and replaced, the traditional mythology will continue and may over time infuse the Christian practices with meanings from the traditional religion.

A fourth key element in order to avoid syncretism is to provide a recorded "oral Bible" for each people group in their language. This is a recorded set of stories, biblically accurate and told in the worldview context. At this point the "oral Bible" may be the only scriptural resource available to oral learners. At some future time when written Bible translation is completed, then it could be recorded to provide a standard point of reference.

In an "oral Bible," the stories are communicated in natural, live situations by mother tongue "storyers" from the people group, using the mannerisms and storytelling techniques which are appropriate to that people group. The Bible stories are checked to ensure biblical accuracy before recording takes place. By utilizing this system that checks the stories as they are told, it will ensure that this recorded "oral Bible" is a plumb line for oral methods such as stories, song, etc.

By telling Bible stories in a straightforward way, we give new converts an opportunity to engage biblical truth directly and discover its message for themselves. This approach is significantly different from the approach that has people read numerous individual verses sequenced according to the

---

24   Detailed examples and training resources on how to conduct a worldview study can be found on the website www.chronologicalbiblestorying.com

curriculum writer's sense of importance and logic and largely divorced from their biblical context. Telling a biblical story in an interesting and accurate way is a simple but powerful manner of freeing disciples to process Scripture. They can do it with a minimum of filtering and interpretive baggage coming from the discipler's culture and experience of Christianity. This is especially true when we tell the stories in chronological order, thus putting them in a biblical context.

The practice of keeping the story *pure* (separate from our own comments and interpretive remarks) protects the oral learners from the syncretism that might come from embracing a polished system of ethics, theology or pastoral philosophy that has a significant dose of European, North American, Korean, Brazilian or Chinese cultural baggage. Instead they synthesize a biblical theology from the stories and can apply it in all kinds of practical situations with courage.

In summary, those of us who seek to make disciples of oral learners will want them to understand biblical truth and live obedient lives as free from syncretism as possible. We can increase the likelihood of that happening when we disciple in the mother tongue, use worldview-specific approaches instead of generic ones, utilize biblical stories extensively and work with mother-tongue speakers to produce an "oral Bible" that provides a reliable repository of biblical truth.

5

reproducibility,
reproducibility,
reproducibility

Reproducibility, Reproducibility, Reproducibility

M ANY people accept the idea that an oral approach like chronological Bible storying may be appropriate to initial evangelism, but they wonder whether a storying approach is viable for a sustained, indigenous-led church planting movement. Is it adequate for sustained discipleship among second, third and successive generations and for leadership development in the church? Those working in storying in face-to-face, relational societies assert that not only is it a viable approach to meet these needs—it is the preferred approach to ensure reproducibility and thus sustainability in an emerging, indigenous-led church.

For a spiritual movement to be engaged, we must consciously choose strategies that oral learners can easily reproduce. We must constantly evaluate whether we are modeling the kind of disciples we want the learners to become. This is the most powerful form of discipling. Oral communicators learn best when they pattern themselves after those who led them to Christ. From our first contact with non-Christians, we are modeling how a Christian relates to non-Christians and seeks to introduce them to Jesus Christ. Thus even our evangelism is in this sense a part of discipling.

The first and most basic aspect of ensuring reproducibility in a storying approach is crafting and telling stories in a way that the hearers are able to readily learn and tell themselves and thus effect a reproducing evangelism. This is why we place great importance on the live, natural telling of stories by mother tongue storyers in the common situations where people communicate with one another. When the gospel is communicated to an oral learner in a way that shows dependence on a written or recorded presentation, it inhibits this reproducibility.

A storyer from Senegal reported:

> Recently one of the oral learners told all of us the story of Cain and Abel. She was very accurate, animated, and told all of it from memory. She also led the discussion time with questions. The truly amazing part is that she had missed the previous week's lesson and had learned the story at midweek prayer meeting from another woman who had been present for the training. This oral learner had learned the story from one who had herself just learned the story and had learned to tell it. Some of their children who attend the study with them have prayed: 'Thank You that our mother is now able to teach us the Bible.' [25]

A similar case is reported among the Santal people of South Asia.[26] Village literacy among this people group was found to be 0.08%. The Santal people have no written history and do not rely on written documents for evidence or for credibility. They rely on what the elders have decided or what the elders say. A Christian outreach effort went to a Santal village and met Marandi, a man who had never been to school. They presented the gospel using oral methods, including stories, visual aids, dramas, songs, dances, and testimonies. Marandi trusted Christ and shared his testimony with his family, who also believed and were baptized. He then went to other relatives and shared his new faith with them, using many

---

25   From http://www.chronologicalbiblestorying.com/news/newsletters, Oct 2001, Vol. 8, No 4.

26   This account is provided by S. D. Ponraj and Sheila Ponraj

of the same oral methods. They also believed and were baptized. He then formed a team of believers, all oral communicators, who went to neighbouring villages using the same combination of stories, dramas, songs, etc. People in those villages accepted Christ, too. Those new believers formed their own teams and they went to yet other villages, still using the same basic strategies that had been introduced in the beginning. Many Santal people believed and they then formed their own outreach teams. The movement continues today among the Santal people.

Other stories and case studies attest that discipling, church planting and developing leaders are also effectively done by a storying approach. First consider a story that shows effective discipling within an oral, storying approach.

In a dusty village in southwestern Nigeria, "Timothy" serves faithfully as pastor of a young church consisting of Yoruba farmers and their families.[27] Three years into his pastorate, Timothy had the opportunity to attend a short course for pastors on chronological Bible storying. There he learned the ancient way of teaching that was new to him. He was encouraged to tell Bible stories in an accurate and interesting way and then lead the group to retell the story, discuss its meaning, and relate the truths to their lives. Upon arriving home, Timothy decided that on the following Sunday he would try out what he had learned.

Because the conference leader had recommended telling Bible stories in chronological sequence, Timothy decided to begin with the story of the creation of spirit beings. He drew on several biblical passages to formulate this particular story as had been illustrated in the short course. After asking them about their creation stories and getting no response, Timothy told the Yoruba creation story. He used that as a bridge to the biblical narration of the story of the creation of angelic beings. He presented it as a story—without explaining it or exhorting the group. Afterward, he asked for someone to retell the biblical story and someone did. Then he asked them questions and led in a dialogue that helped them understand and apply the story.

---

27   This account is provided by Grant Lovejoy.

"It was thrilling to me that someone was able to tell the story and others made corrections," he later reported. "The people were very eager to hear more of the stories. When they began to ask questions that were beyond the story, I did not answer [their questions] but simply told them, 'as I tell more stories, you will discover that yourself.'"

Timothy explained, "I have come to understand that they are more open to ask questions with this method, unlike when I was using the [denominational] Sunday School book. Even the children were answering questions. So it is good for the children too. I have decided to train someone by sharing the story on Saturday with the person so that he or she can share with the children on Sunday.

"I also discovered as I asked them questions and listened to their questions that they were still holding on to their previous teachings of worshipping angels," Timothy explained. "To them the angels are from heaven and can reach God better, so we can pass through them to God. This session has further taught me that they have not understood my topical sermons. It now gives me the opportunity to explain to them things on this issue which I do not normally preach on."

Timothy used the same approach the next Sunday, telling the story of the creation of the heavens and the earth. After this second storying session with them, he commented, "Some of their questions during the session have made me understand that they have not understood many things from the Bible for these three years [that he had been their pastor]."

Timothy discovered several important lessons about making disciples. He realized that to effectively disciple, one must first determine how one's people learn. Although Timothy had pastored his people for three years, he had not been aware that his preaching style needed to match the people's learning style.

They lived in a relational culture with a strong oral tradition. They passed on their history in stories and proverbs. Timothy became conscious of the fact that he was a literate pastor trained in literate teaching methods. The methods he had been taught to use worked well among people highly educated in western schools, but they didn't work well in his situation. He decided to return to his cultural roots as well as model his preaching and teaching after the greatest teacher—Jesus.

Before Timothy changed his teaching methods, he had been frustrated by his people's lack of response. He thought the problem was theirs, that perhaps they were not very intelligent. When Timothy changed his methods the people responded and he discerned that he had been the problem because he had not been communicating effectively. He said, "I have learned to be patient with learners and not to condemn them rashly when they give some 'stupid' answers that are not relevant to what we are discussing. This has encouraged most that didn't use to respond to questions to do so now."

An oral, storying approach can likewise be effective for church planting. A recent church planting movement took place in South Asia among a highly oral people.[28] The oral peoples consisted of various scheduled castes, some of whom were animists while others were of Hindu religious background. From 1997-2003 an agricultural project combined with a chronological Bible storying approach led to approximately two thousand new church starts. An expatriate strategy coordinator worked with two media specialists—one a national and one an expatriate—to develop the biblical stories and the communications strategies. The stories were chosen and crafted with biblical accuracy to engage the people at their worldview values and beliefs level. The stories that were told in the villages were the same stories they heard through the FEBA radio broadcasts. The media specialist and FEBA provided taped recordings that served to improve the hearers' memory of the stories. The local Christian farmers, who were trained in implementing vital agricultural and health technologies, mentored other farmers even on large plantations.

---

28   This account is provided by James B. Slack.

In using those technologies, they told the Bible stories in sequence in the evenings after the agriculture sessions. Those who demonstrated further interest in the Bible stories they heard were invited into Bible story listening groups focused on the radio broadcasts. In the groups they would hear the stories told again but in those groups they were organized to discuss the stories as they heard them. Later the stories were also told face to face by those who became interested in the stories and who embraced Jesus Christ as Lord and Saviour. Again, the stories were circulated on audiocassette. It is important to understand that the stories heard on the radio, the stories told in the fields and villages, and the stories heard on the cassettes were the same stories.

Thousands of believers have come from this wedding of agricultural, health and storytelling technologies. As this church planting movement continues to escalate through these partner methods, the locals are now addressing aberrant doctrinal beliefs through stories. An independent evaluation of this situation revealed a situation where the lay pastors discipled and trained by oral methods maintained essentially correct doctrine, compared to more literate pastors in the same people group, trained by literate means, who exhibited syncretized doctrinal positions. This group dates its origin to a preacher who came in the 1760s. They had about 250 churches when the multiplication of churches began through the storying approaches. Since they began storying, they have gone from a mathematical average of approximately one new church a year to approximately one new church a day.

Another example of church planting using similar storying strategies comes from Romania.[29] Expatriate church planting strategists with the Deaf were involved in a storying approach with associates in planting five Deaf churches. Those among the Romanian Deaf community who became believers through a storying approach in those five church plants went on to plant twenty more Deaf churches. They used the telling of their own testimonies in their heart language, Romanian Sign Language, coupled with chronological Bible storying.

---

29   This account is provided by Doc Douglas and Dee Douglas.

Deaf communities have many of the same features that characterize oral communicators. In fact, a more comprehensive way of looking at what are called "orality" features is not that they are crucially or exclusively associated with what is spoken by mouth. They are, instead a correlation of ways of processing

that are common to face-to-face, highly relational societies. The correlation of ways of processing and communicating involve concrete (rather than abstract) notions; sequential (rather than random) expression of events; and relational (as opposed to individualist) contexts. Both oral cultures and Deaf communities exhibit these characteristics because

they are face-to-face, highly relational cultures. Throughout the world, Deaf communities are being reached by chronological Bible storying methods. So there is reason to include them in this discussion. (It is in some sense inaccurate to call the Deaf "oral communicators." Furthermore, they dislike the terms "oral," "orality" and "oralism" because they associate the terms with nineteenth and twentieth century efforts to force the Deaf to give up sign language and learn to speak.)

An account of oral, storying strategies that were effective in leadership development comes from North Africa.[30] There 17 young men (many of whom could barely read and write and some not at all) underwent a two-year leader training program using chronological Bible storying. At the end of two years, students mastered approximately 135 biblical stories in their correct chronological order, spanning from Genesis to Revelation. They

---

30   This account is provided by Grant Lovejoy.

were able to tell the stories, sing from one to five songs for each story, and enact dramas about each of the stories. A seminary professor gave them a six-hour oral exam. They demonstrated the ability to answer questions about both the facts and theology of the stories and showed an excellent grasp of the gospel message, the nature of God, and their new life in Christ. The students quickly and skillfully referred to the stories to answer a variety of theological questions. Given a theological theme, they could accurately name multiple biblical stories in which that theme occurs. If asked, they could tell each story and elaborate on how it addressed the theme.

The professor concluded that "the training process has successfully achieved its goals of enabling students to tell a large number of biblical stories accurately, to have a good understanding of those stories and the theology that they convey and to have an eagerness to share the Christian message. The community received the stories and story-songs enthusiastically and have made them part of the culture and church life alike."

"Various students acknowledged that they entered knowing little of the Old Testament, did not understand the relationship between God and Jesus, did not know the characteristics of God, did not know that God created the angelic beings, had not heard of being born again and did not know that Christians should not seek help from local deities. Upon entering the program these students were unable to communicate the Christian faith to other people, but by the time the training was over, they had dramatically improved their understanding of all of these matters and many more," he said. The songs and stories became so popular that when the students returned to their villages, the local people eagerly gathered to learn the new songs and stories, and frequently sang the Scripture songs and told the stories late into the night, sometimes even until dawn.

The stories and case studies above illustrate various aspects of reproducibility among relational-narrative communicators, both among oral communicators and the Deaf. One important aspect of this involves them telling the story of their own experience of coming to faith in Christ. Those from face-to-face societies readily testify to their personal, daily relationship with Christ. Testimony times in worship services in Western services are limited or non-existent. However, among oral communicators, testimony and prayer times may take up most of the service. When friends and neighbours hear these testimonies and see the change in new converts' lives, they often want to follow the "Jesus road." After they have come to Christ through a process of biblical revelation through stories, the discipler helps them learn an abridged story of the gospel message to use immediately. Disciplers then encourage them to give others the opportunity to hear the biblical stories they heard, in order to consolidate their faith and give these new believers a biblical foundation. Multiple church planting and discipleship efforts from the U. S. to China now incorporate a "my story, your story, God's story, others' stories approach."

Discipling oral communicators involves identifying what the new believers need to know and do and then communicating these truths using appropriate methods. These methods include modeling, telling a Bible story that communicates a truth, discussing it, perhaps memorizing a Scripture related to the matter and applying the truth together or individually. Their discipleship is shaped by the modeling of another believer and on-the-job training. This is most effective when the modeling is done by an in-culture or close-culture believer. Discipleship is not just what one does but who one is—a new creature in Christ. Then we must help them understand that discipleship is primarily a matter of obedience to everything Jesus commanded and revealed in Scripture.

Discipling involves having the disciple do all of the preceding plus being held accountable to report back. This model of discipleship emphasizes accountability for application in two crucial dimensions: living it and sharing it with others. Oral learners, like all true followers of Jesus, need to practice what Scripture teaches and to pass along to others what they are learning.

Oral communicators are more dependent on relationships in communication than literate learners are. For that reason oral communicators tend to place a higher value on those relationships. They believe persons more than abstract truths. So the spiritual life and modeling of the messenger is crucial. Making disciples of oral communicators requires maintaining a loving relationship with the ones being discipled. Disciplers help oral communicators acquire biblical truth through appropriate oral means and guide them to obey it. Disciplers also teach them to win and disciple others who will in turn disciple others. The new converts join existing churches or form new churches, according to the situation.

Discipling oral communicators should lead directly to church planting as new converts come together in covenant communities of believers to carry out the functions of the church. In many instances, these will be house churches that develop along lines of kinship and friendship. Disciples grow best when, from the beginning of their Christian experience, they take responsibility for evangelizing, nurturing new converts, establishing new works and overseeing the development of their own converts.

Providing orally based leader training for oral learners and equipping them to continue it within their people group is one of the great challenges facing the Church. Those involved in rapidly growing church planting movements must disciple and equip leaders for the new churches as leaders are raised up by the Holy Spirit. If they do not, the expansion of the movement slows or ceases.

A summarization of the storying approach from the CD series, *Following Jesus: Making Disciples of Oral Learners*, specifies a ten-step process toward making disciples of primary oral learners with reproducibility as the important culminating step:

- *Identify* the biblical principle that you want to communicate – simply and clearly.
- *Evaluate* the worldview issues of the chosen people group.

49

- *Consider* worldview – the bridges, barriers, and gaps.
- *Select* the biblical stories that are needed to communicate the biblical principle.
- *Plan* (craft) the story and plan the dialogue that is going to follow the story, focusing on the task to be accomplished.
- *Communicate* the story in a culturally appropriate way, using narrative, song, dance, object lessons, and other forms.
- *Apply* the principle by facilitating dialogue with the group, helping them to discover the meaning and application of the story to their own lives.
- *Obey* the discovered principle by implementation steps to be taken by the individuals.
- *Accountability* – establish accountability between group members by mutual and reciprocal commitments to implement the biblical principle in the conduct of their personal lives between members of the group, their families and other personal relationships.
- *Reproduce* – encourage the group to reproduce the biblical principle, first by demonstrating the principle in their own "witness of life" then in sharing the principle with others. [31]

Bible storying provides a way of engaging a people group that is not highly technological and can readily involve oral communicators in efforts to reach their own people group with the gospel. Storying is thus a reproducible evangelistic and church planting approach—new believers can readily share the gospel, plant new churches and disciple new believers in the same way that they themselves were reached and discipled.

While a storying strategy seems to be one that is particularly appropriate with unreached people groups, many involved with people groups where there is an established church have found significant benefits to a chronological storying approach in those situations as well. The oral, chronological approach can fill major gaps that literate approaches to evangelism,

---

31   *Following Jesus: Making Disciples of Primary Oral Learners*, hosted by Avery T. Willis Jr., Progressive Vision, 2002.

discipling, church planting and leadership development have, over the decades, missed.

6

when literates

stop
reading

When Literates
Stop Reading

RECALL the statement that two-thirds of the world's people can't, won't, or don't read and write. The bulk of this paper has focused on those who can't. This part will focus on those who don't. These are those who choose to learn by oral methods as opposed to literate ones, in spite of their literacy. These people are known as secondary oral learners. James B. Slack defines "secondary oral learners" as "people who have become literate because of their job or schooling, but prefer to be entertained, learn and communicate by oral means." Walter Ong, father of the modern orality movement, says, "I style the orality of a culture totally untouched by writing or print, 'primary orality.' It is 'primary' by contrast with the 'secondary orality' of present-day high-technology culture, in which a new orality is sustained by telephone, radio, television and other electronic devices that depend for their existence and functioning on writing and print."[32]

Earlier in this paper we explored the characteristics of oral learners. It is increasingly evident that many of these same characteristics are as descriptive of secondary oral learners as they are of primary oral learners. As such, the effectiveness of our communication is dependent on what we do with this knowledge.

---

32   Ong, Walter J. *Orality & Literacy: The Technologizing of the World* (London and New York: Routledge, 1982).

Our purpose is to call missions-minded Christians to explore ways to be more effective in communicating with secondary oral learners—in reaching them for Christ, helping them grow and mobilizing them to involvement in ministry.

Why is it important to do this? A 2004 study reported that "literary reading in America is not only declining rapidly among all groups, but the rate of decline has accelerated, especially among the young." This reflects a "massive shift toward electronic media for entertainment and information."[33] Numerous western societies are seeing similar shifts toward electronic media and the accompanying secondary orality.

Consider the following statistics:

• 58% of the U. S. adult population never read another book after high school.

• 42% of U. S. university graduates never read another book.

• Adults in the U. S. spend four hours per day watching TV, three hours listening to the radio and 14 minutes reading magazines.[34]

• British teenagers' pleasure reading declined by about a third from 1991-1998.[35]

• In Denmark one-third of adults do not do any significant amount of reading.[36]

• More than half the adults in the Netherlands hardly ever read a book.[37]

---

33   *Reading at Risk: A Survey of Literary Reading in America,* Research Division Report no. 46 (Washington, DC: National Endowment for the Arts, 2004), vii. The term "literary reading" includes books such as romance novels, so these statistics reflect pleasure reading generally, not just the reading of "literary classics." The survey included 17,000 adults and was administered by the U. S. Census Bureau.

34   The first three items are reported by Dan Poynter and cited in http://newwway. org/news/2004/apr 2.htm.

35   *Young People in 1998,* a report compiled from surveys of 18,221 pupils by the Schools Health Education Unit based at Exeter University. Available at http://www. sheu.org.uk/pubs/yp98.htm.

36   Viggo Sogaard, *Evangelizing Our World: Insights from Global Inquiry* (Pattaya, Thailand: 2004 Forum for World Evangelization, 2004), 11.

37   Both statements about reading in the Netherlands are from Marieke Sanders-

- Dutch 12 year old school children spend, on average, less than half an hour a week reading in their leisure time.

Apparently, related trends are unfolding elsewhere in the world.

"Reading and writing are clearly dying arts," professor Jim Dator of the University of Hawaii said, "something which fewer in the world are doing." More important, he said, is the fact that reading and writing are something fewer and fewer people need to know how to do. "Most people in the world, even most of the literate people in the world in fact, do not get much of their ideas about the world from reading. They get them from watching television, going to the movies, listening to the radio, and other forms of audio-visual communication."[38]

Ravi Zacharias, a Christian apologist, agrees. "More and more we are knowing less and less about the printed tradition," he said. "The ability for abstract reasoning is diminishing in our time, because [people] come to their conclusions on the basis of images. Their capacity for abstract reasoning i s gone." Zacharias concludes that we are now in a time where there is a "humiliation of the word" and an "exaltation of the image."[39]

In their book *Church Next: Quantum Changes in Christian Ministry*, Eddie Gibbs and Ian Coffey also conclude that people today are more influenced by audio and visual media than print

---

ten Holte, "Creating an Optimum Reading Culture in the Low Countries: The Role of Stichting Lezen," a paper presented at the 64th International Federation of Library Associations and Institutions General Conference, Aug.16-21, 1998, Amsterdam, http://www.ifla.org/IV/ifla64/098-80e.htm.

38   Jim Dator, "Families, Communities, and Futures," http://www.soc.hawaii.edu/future/dator/other/FCF.html

39   Ravi Zacharias, "Mind Games in a World of Images," audiotape.

media. "Theirs is a post-literacy culture for which sound and image have largely replaced the printed word," they claim. The two argue that "instancy" and intimacy are the distinguishing features of today's non-print media, and that seeing, not reading, is the basis for believing.[40]

Pritish Nandi, publisher and television news producer in India, recently wrote an article titled "Will Technology Usher in an Era of Illiteracy?" In it he said, "New technology will no longer divide the world into literate and illiterate people but will bring everyone together in a common platform where the ability to read and write will no longer matter. You will have a new world where people will need an entirely different kind of skills set to succeed."[41]

All of these examples are clear indications of a growing global emergence of secondary orality, or post-literacy as some call it. This phenomenon is causing us to think, communicate, process information, and make decisions more and more like oral peoples. The implications of this have ramifications not only on what we do in evangelism, discipleship, leader training and church planting, but also on how we do it! We must make adjustments in the way we communicate the message of the gospel, acknowledging that our goal, responsibility, and desire are to communicate truth in the most effective ways possible.

For many of us, it is becoming more and more evident that issues of secondary orality are reaching the very altars of our churches around the world. Christian researcher George Barna said that technology and the mass media have forever changed the ways in which we process information, saying that "the inability to systematically apply scriptural truth produces a spiritual superficiality or immaturity that is reflected in behaviour." He concludes that we must develop new forums and formats through which people will experience, understand, and serve God.[42]

---

40 Eddie Gibbs and Ian Coffey, *Church Next: Quantum Changes in Christian Ministry* (Leicester, England: Inter-Varsity Press, 2001), 127.
41 *The International Indian*, 9:4, (August 2001), 22.
42 George Barna, *The Second Coming of the Church: A Blue Print for Survival* (Nashville: Word Publishing, 1998).

Tommy Jones, author of *Postmodern Youth Ministry,* urges us to tell stories. "Narrative is becoming the primary means of telling beliefs. Since propositional logic has fallen on hard times, stories carry more weight in carrying truths – "abductive" reasoning. As opposed to deductive or inductive methods, when you tell a story, you 'abduct' listeners from their known worlds into another world."[43]

Rick Durst, academic dean at Golden Gate Seminary in California, agrees. "To be a 'storyteller' is no longer a euphemism for someone with a loose grip on truth," he said. "The storyteller is becoming again the person of wisdom who knows the 'good telling stories' that make and maintain community and meaning." Durst refers to well-known Christian author Leonard Sweet, who sees pastors as "story doctors," who use the "truthing" of biblical stories to heal the dysfunctional stories confining and confounding people's lives, concluding that ministry to the emerging generation will be magnified to the degree that narrative is applied.[44]

How do we get started? First, we need to pray that God will show us how to be more effective. We need to ask for ways to turn what have been barriers into bridges. Second, we need to be observant of what is already proven in how to communicate with literate people who have at least some preference for learning orally. For example, many graduate programs in business administration use case study discussions to teach essential leadership principles. As another example, many of the most effective evangelistic speakers and pastors use stories to illustrate their message points. Dallas Theological Seminary professor Howard Hendricks is quoted as saying that such illustrations are the windows to the soul. As a third example, many who teach the Bible in small groups have discovered that a way to understanding is for the student to see specifically how a Bible truth looks when it is applied. If the leader is able to share his or her own experience (story) with how this works, learning is greatly accelerated.

---

43   Tommy Jones, *Postmodern Youth Ministry* (Grand Rapids: Zondervan, 2001), 27.
44   Jones, 27.

Summarizing this second point, we already know a lot about using oral methods with people who are literate. We just need to surface what we know and become more intentional in using it.

Finally, we must proactively experiment with new ways to be even better in communicating with secondary oral learners. One such experiment is being done in Orlando, Florida, by Campus Crusade for Christ. A group of Christian college students are being taught how to do follow-up and discipleship using storying versus using written materials. Four types of stories are being used by the disciplers:

- God's stories (narratives from Scripture)
- Their stories (stories of the discipler's own experience with God)
- Others' stories (stories from other people's lives and video clips from movies and TV programs)
- Disciples' stories (immediate practical applications of biblical truth so that the new disciple can develop his or her own stories that can be used to minister to others, thus promoting spiritual multiplication)

Similar models are being launched with executives and professionals, as well as with new Christians in Sunday School classes.

These are but a beginning of the kinds of extensive and innovative efforts that will be necessary to learn how to use storying to connect better with secondary oral learners of all educational and socioeconomic levels. As lessons are learned, they need to be shared freely to further accelerate the learning process in how to be more effective.

We possess knowledge of the greatest story ever told. We increasingly understand how to communicate that knowledge better with the two-thirds of the population of earth who will receive it best through storying and other oral means. In recent years we have begun to see that storying can greatly increase effectiveness even with literate people, including college students and business and professional people.

Our call to action is simple: Let's do everything we can to set aside any tendencies we might have to ignore or not utilize this fact, and let's pray and take advantage of every effective method so that, in the spirit of the apostle Paul, "by all possible means we might save some."

7
a.
growing
engagement

A Growing Engagement

ASPECTS of the storying approach are still under development and orality is still a relatively young academic discipline. Even so, there is enough confidence in the effectiveness of oral approaches to making disciples that reputable organizations are investing resources in an ever-growing engagement of the approach. Following are several examples reflecting this growing movement.[45]

The International Mission Board (IMB) of the Southern Baptist Convention, the largest denominational international mission agency, is heavily engaged in this approach. IMB has hundreds of field teams using storying as a primary strategy in dozens of countries. In Suriname a storying strategy in one people group enabled Christianity to spread from a handful of known believers to the point of having believers living in every village in that people group in less than five years. Most villages also have a house church.

Scriptures In Use (SIU) and local partners, such as Bihar Outreach Network in India and many others around the globe, have trained over 7000 grassroots workers in 50 countries in

---

45 Many of these ministries produce training and ministry resources. See the Resources section for more information about them and for contact information.

Communication Bridges to Oral Cultures. This short course equips non-Western workers to understand their own oral cultures and to develop Scripture storying skills and strategies such as storytelling-drama, cultural adaptations of Scripture in song, memorization, and recitation. SIU focuses on mentoring other agencies through the process of adopting oral methods into their missions programs in order to address orality and the needs of oral cultures within their regions of influence. In one area 75 churches have been planted with 1450 believers, in another area 30 churches were planted in two years; and in another difficult area 22 churches were planted in three years.

Over the past six years, an alliance of international agencies which has come to be known as the International Orality Network has sponsored consultations aimed at sharing insights and experiences in orality and storying and promoting the approach. Sponsoring agencies include Campus Crusade for Christ (CCC), Faith Comes by Hearing, God's Story, Grass Roots Church Planters, IMB, Progressive Vision, Scriptures In Use, Southwestern Baptist Theological Seminary, Trans World Radio (TWR), The Navigators, visionSynergy, Wycliffe International, YWAM (Youth With A Mission).

Table 71, a partnership growing out of Amsterdam 2000, involving the leadership of CCC, Discipling A Whole Nation (DAWN), IMB, WorldTeach, Wycliffe and YWAM, has adopted chronological Bible storying as a primary strategy of cooperative efforts.

Progressive Vision has recently produced *Following Jesus: Making Disciples of Oral Learners*, (2002) an orally-based discipleship resource. *Following Jesus* models the practice of identifying a biblical truth that should be taught, inquiring how the people group would perceive that truth through their worldview, and then selecting biblical stories that could be used to teach that truth in light of that worldview. It consists of seven modules of 53 audio CDs that teach how to communicate to oral learners. The modules give the format and tell over 400 Bible stories that enable the oral learner to go from being a new Christian to becoming a senior pastor or cross-cultural missionary without having to read.

OneStory,[46] a partnership founded by CCC, IMB, Wycliffe and YWAM, is engaging a storying approach among unreached peoples. OneStory conducts training and workshops and establishes OneStory training centers around the world to enable churches or agencies to prepare forty to fifty initial stories in an unreached people's language, equipping mother-tongue storyers to tell the stories and multiply churches. It also makes audio recordings of the stories for archiving and broad sowing by volunteers.

Radio ministries are becoming increasingly involved in supporting oral approaches. FEBA Radio has partnered with other agencies in Central Asia, the Middle East and North Africa in broadcasting stories. TWR has recently identified orality as one of five top strategic initiatives.

A Deaf Bible Network has been formed fostering Deaf nationals recording Bible stories in their native sign languages: *God's Stories in Sign*. Deaf Opportunity Out Reach (DOOR) has four training sites for chronological Bible storying where Deaf leaders from over 25 countries have been trained.

Global Recordings Network (GRN, formerly Gospel Recordings) has produced audio and audio-visual Bible-based evangelism and discipling resources in more than 5500 languages designed specifically for non- and minimally-literate people groups. These resources continue to be refined as GRN develops strategic partnerships with other like-minded organizations to reach the unreached oral communicators of the world.

This growing engagement is not limited to missions agencies. Local churches are getting involved as well. Larry Johnson is a coordinator among pastors in Ellis County, Texas, a rural county south of Dallas.[47] Johnson attended a training event about oral

---

46   The original name for the OneStory Partnership was Epic Partners, International. The name was changed to avoid confusion with other ministries and organizations. The name of the partnership has been updated throughout this book.

47   This account is provided by James B. Slack.

communicators and how to work effectively with them. There he realized that there were many oral communicators in his county and came to understand how the churches could minister to them more effectively. When he returned to Ellis County, he shared his findings with pastors. "They recognized that these are the people they are not reaching through traditional churches," he said. "They may be members, but they are not in positions of leadership and are probably on the fringes."

Johnson then enlisted pastors, interested educators, church members, and other skilled people to identify worldview values and beliefs among Ellis county oral communicators. They then chose biblical stories to speak to the oral peoples' view of the world, crafted them, and set about to test them through telling them to sample groups of oral people in the county. They also selected visual materials to use in conjunction with the stories. They have set a goal of planting 700 churches, most of which will meet in homes.

While making these preparations, Johnson heard through international missions announcements that leaders in Central America needed churches to partner with them in evangelizing a specific unreached people group. Today these local churches in Ellis County have gotten additional training in language and worldview issues, and have extended their use of oral strategies to Central America. Johnson comments: "We are now doing overseas among an oral people group what we have been learning to do among our own oral people in Ellis County."

Strategies using oral methods, then, are not unproven theories. They have a proven track record, beginning with biblical times and continuing to the present. Under a wide array of situations, among diverse people groups on virtually every continent, oral strategies have demonstrated their effectiveness in evangelism, discipleship, church planting, and leader development.

What can an individual do to become a part of this growing engagement in making disciples among oral learners? Here are some practical steps: Any individual reading this paper can learn more about the field of orality and storying by reading the books, visiting the websites, or contacting the agencies referenced in this paper. The individual can learn to story passages from the Bible. The individual can identify the nearby oral communicators who are not believers and look for natural opportunities to story the gospel among them and to disciple them with stories. Individuals can share their journey in storying with the local church they are part of, and investigate ways of going global like those in Ellis County have done.

Conclusions

From the time of the Gutenberg Bible, Christianity "has walked on literate feet." Christians have led the literacy movement because of desiring to read the Bible for themselves. Yet Christians increasingly are concerned that hundreds of years have passed without a comprehensive global Kingdom advance. In 2,000 years since Christ's Great Commission, only about 10% of all peoples are evangelical followers of Jesus.

Effective discipling of oral learners allows them to embrace biblical patterns of Christian life and belief and utilize communication forms that are familiar within the culture. Of necessity, discipling oral learners involves communicating the unchanging message of Scripture into varied and ever-changing cultures in worldview-sensitive ways. It means discipling in ways designed to avoid creating dependency on the discipler. It means setting the oral disciples free to evangelize, disciple, plant churches and train leaders in a never-ceasing pattern. Only then will the message be able to reach to "the uttermost parts of the earth."

So what shall we do with this fresh insight to communicate with oral learners? This is an issue for the Lausanne Committee for World Evangelization (LCWE) and the entire Christian world to investigate, embrace, propagate and utilize in finishing the task of reaching the unreached peoples of the world. Here are proposed actions:

1. The LCWE to highlight this issue as essential for the evangelization of the world, especially the unreached people groups.

2. The LCWE endorse a "Lausanne Task Force on Making Disciples of Oral Learners" to explore and implement all

practical means to advance the cause of making disciples of
oral learners worldwide.

3.   The LCWE and others to publish material to permeate
the missions world with information about oral strategies.

4.   Churches and other Christian organizations to develop and
implement methods, communications, and strategies such as:

   a.   Local churches becoming advocates for specific
   unreached people groups and promoting an engagement
   with those people groups by using worldview-specific oral
   methodologies.

   b.   Seminaries providing curricula to train pastors and
   missionaries in oral methodologies.

   c.   Local churches around the world utilizing oral
   methodologies to disciple their own members as a way of
   avoiding syncretism.

   d.   Mission agencies developing strategies for their
   missionaries and partners to use among oral learners.

   e.   Regional networks hosting conferences in strategic
   locations around the world for awareness building about
   oral methodologies.

   f.   Regional partnerships and agencies providing training
   in strategic locations to train local leaders and missionaries
   in implementing oral strategies among the unreached.

   g.   Regional partnerships and agencies developing a network
   of trainers to train other trainers in oral methodologies.

   h.   Churches and agencies recording and distributing Bible
   stories for evangelization, discipling, and leader training.

   i.   Broadcast networks and agencies broadcasting
   chronological Bible stories and recordings of a discipleship
   group in a house church setting, including dialogue
   reflecting culturally appropriate ways of processing the
   story and interacting with it.

   j.   Funding organizations making resources available for
   oral methodologies to be implemented with the thousands
   of language groups, people groups, and segments of societies
   that are still unreached.

With the insights gleaned from research and collaboration, Christians have the opportunity to reach in our generation the billions of unreached people in the world headed to a Christless eternity. Following the example of Jesus' own witness through parables and proverbs, we can communicate the gospel orally in a way that these unreached people can understand, respond to, and reproduce. Let us therefore go forth embracing oral communicators as partners—together making disciples of all peoples to the glory of God!

executive
summary
▽

FROM the time of the Gutenberg Bible, Christianity "has walked on literate feet" and has directly or indirectly required literacy of others. However, two-thirds of all people in the world are oral communicators—those who can't, don't, or won't learn through literate means. Four billion in our world are at risk of a Christless eternity unless literate Christians make significant changes in evangelism, discipleship, leader training and church planting.

Making disciples of oral learners means using communication forms that are familiar within the culture: stories, proverbs, drama, songs, chants, and poetry. Literate approaches rely on lists, outlines, word studies, apologetics and theological jargon. These literate methods are largely ineffective among two-thirds of the world's peoples. Of necessity, making disciples of oral learners depends on communicating God's word with varied cultures in relevant ways. Only then will the gospel be able to reach to "the uttermost parts of the earth."

Key Issues for the Church to Address:

Five aspects of making disciples of oral learners in the context of the Great Commission must be considered vital to "finishing the task":

1. Make the word of God available to unreached peoples using appropriate oral strategies.

The church is commanded by Christ to "make disciples of all peoples" which certainly includes the vast majority of the yet unreached oral learners. Providing an "oral Bible" allows God's word to be produced accurately from memory for the purpose of re-telling. The "oral Bible" is the singular key to unlocking church planting movements among unreached people groups. However, that "oral Bible" must penetrate the people group to its worldview level belief system. Only then will a Bible become meaningful and useful. The only Bible that will be effective during the lifetime of the vast majority of unreached people is an "oral Bible," probably best presented in narrative form. It is important for the church to understand that a written version of Scripture does not even exist for the majority of languages. Even if literacy were achieved, the Bible would still not exist in some 4,000 languages (see further in Chapter 2 below).

2. Use oral communication patterns which allow the whole community to hear clearly in their mother tongue, to understand, respond and reproduce the message of the gospel.

Literate church leaders and their missionaries should master new ways of preaching and teaching. Effective ministries among those with an oral learning preference will use communication forms already in place within their own culture. If the gospel is to spread freely and rapidly within an unreached people group, strategists working in that group must do their best to avoid methodology that hinders oral peoples from winning and discipling their own families, friends and others. Training models will be most effective when they take orality into consideration. Churches will then begin to see training and new leaders emerge from within the oral peoples. These leaders will facilitate church-planting movements to rapidly disciple and equip leaders for the new churches as leaders are raised up by the Holy Spirit.

3. Avoid syncretism by making disciples of oral learners using oral means.

If the church is going to avoid syncretism, then the gospel needs to be communicated in the mother tongue of the people we are trying to reach. Both evangelistic as well as discipleship materials cannot be generic but will need to be developed with the worldview of the target people. The stories chosen and the manner in which they are communicated will have to transform the worldview of those who are seeing or hearing the stories. A recorded oral Bible will help serve as a standard to ensure the transmission of the stories remains accurate. These methods will help ensure the church remains true to the historic beliefs of Christianity and does not mix traditional beliefs in their doctrines or practices.

4. Equip relational-narrative communicators to make disciples.

Oral strategies provide multiple ways for effectively engaging a people group to readily involve oral communicators in efforts to reach their own people group and others with the gospel. Storying is one reproducible evangelistic and church-planting approach—new believers can readily share the gospel, plant new churches and disciple new believers in the same way that they themselves were reached and discipled.

5. Increase Effectiveness among Secondary Oral Learners.

Oral strategies are also necessary in reaching people whose orality is tied to electronic media. They may be able to read well, but get most of the important information in their lives through stories and music coming through radio, television, film, internet and other electronic means. We need oral strategies focused on this segment of the world population, too.

How Orality Works on the Local Level

While a storying strategy seems to be one that is particularly appropriate with unreached people groups, many established churches, especially in relational cultures, have found significant benefits to the chronological storying approach.

In evangelism: *One missionary couple cautiously entered a West Africa Muslim village.*

> My husband and I asked permission of the village chief to live among the people in order to learn more about them. After living among the people, we asked the chief for permission to share God's word in the village.

He gave us permission to do whatever we wanted. We did not discuss the religion of Christianity or talk about 'the Christian way.' We never discussed Islam, Muhammad or the Quran or the differences between Christianity and Islam. We were there to teach God's word under the leadership of the Holy Spirit. We chose to use only the storying method, to teach the stories of the Bible chronologically and bring out the truths the people needed to know in order to understand the gospel. We began storying in small groups throughout the village and distributed storying cassettes to those who asked. The Imam used some of the stories in his sermons and gave his people permission to listen to the stories. During the next year 20 individuals became followers of Jesus.

In Discipleship: The Puinave people were re-discipled when missionaries discovered syncretism. Although the Puinave had become culturally "Christian" in the 1950s, they mixed magic with Christian do's and don'ts. Many misunderstandings resulted from using the trade language, Spanish. When New Tribes missionaries spent seven years learning the difficult Puinave language in the 1970s, they were surprised at the actual beliefs held among the people. At first, the missionaries tried teaching the Bible using traditional teaching methods. The Puinave nodded their agreement, but obviously missed many of the key points. It was only through a chronological presentation of God's word, Old Testament and on to the Gospels, story by story, that they were able to vividly portray the holy nature and character of God, the sinful condition of man, the grip that Satan has on this world and the redeeming solution to man's predicament found in Jesus Christ. Later, the village elder observed, "I came just this close from going to hell..." holding up his thumb and forefinger. In 1998, New Tribes Mission made this story into a movie titled *Now We See Clearly*.

In Church Leader Training: In a north African Muslim-dominated country, 17 young men (many of whom could barely read and write and some not at all) underwent a two-year leader training program using Chronological Bible Storying. At the end of two years, students mastered approximately 135 biblical stories in their correct chronological order, spanning from Genesis to Revelation. They were able to tell the stories, compose from one to five songs for each story and enact dramas about each of the stories. A seminary professor gave them a six-hour oral exam. They demonstrated the ability to answer questions about both the facts and theology of the stories and showed an excellent grasp of the gospel message, the nature of God and their new life in Christ. The students quickly and skillfully referred to the stories to answer a variety of theological questions.

In Church Planting: In South America, Jeremy, an IMB worker, joined a larger team that included Wycliffe translation workers. Working with stories adapted from a neighbouring language, Jeremy instilled vision for the storying process in two mother tongue storyers and coached them through learning the stories and telling them to others. Jeremy's two-year involvement has been a significant contributing factor toward a church-planting initiative that now has resulted in as many as 20% of the people group becoming believers. In the two years since Jeremy's departure, storyers continue to go to new, unreached villages up and down the river, telling the stories and evangelizing.

These are but a few ways that oral strategies are facilitating God's redemptive work among oral peoples on many continents.

Conclusions, Challenge, and Recommendations

The Lausanne Committee on World Evangelization included "Making Disciples of Oral Learners" as an issue group for the first time in 2004. An estimated 90% of the world's Christian workers work among oral peoples using literate communication styles. Orality issues raise an urgent cry for effectiveness.

What a challenge! Yet, more than *four billion* people in our world need a customized strategy delivered in a culturally appropriate manner in order for them to hear, understand, respond to, and reproduce. The church today must embrace oral communicators as partners—together making disciples of all peoples to the glory of God!

Lausanne's orality issue group challenges churches and other Christian organizations to ride the next wave of Kingdom advancement by developing and implementing methods for effective oral strategies. Partners, networks, seminaries, mission agencies, conference and workshop leaders, as well as other Christian influencers are called upon to recognize the issues of orality in the world around them. We all need to become intentional in making disciples of oral learners. We need to raise awareness, initiate oral communication projects and train missionaries and local leaders in Chronological Bible Storying as an effective church-planting strategy.

We recommend that:

1. The LCWE highlight this issue as essential for the evangelization of the world, especially the unreached people groups.

2. The LCWE endorse a "Lausanne Task Force on Making Disciples of Oral Learners" to explore and implement all practical means to advance the cause of making disciples of oral learners worldwide.

3. The LCWE and others publish material to permeate the missions world with information about oral strategies.

4. Churches and other Christian organizations develop and implement methods, communications and strategies such as:

a. Local churches to become advocates for specific unreached people groups and promote an engagement with those people groups by using worldview-specific oral methodologies.

b. Seminaries to provide curricula to train pastors and missionaries in oral methodologies.

  c. Local churches around the world to utilize oral methodologies as they disciple their own members.

  d. Mission agencies to develop strategies for their missionaries and partners to use among oral learners.

  e. Regional networks to host conferences in strategic locations around the world for awareness building about oral methodologies.

  f. Regional partnerships and agencies to provide training in strategic locations to train local leaders and missionaries in implementing oral strategies among the unreached.

  g. Regional partnerships and agencies to develop a network of trainers to train other trainers in oral methodologies.

  h. Churches and agencies to record and distribute Bible stories for evangelization, discipling and leader training.

  i. Broadcast networks and agencies to broadcast chronological Bible stories and recordings of discipleship groups in house church settings. They should include dialogue which reflects culturally appropriate ways of processing the story and interacting with it.

  j. Funding organizations to make resources available for oral methodologies to be implemented with the thousands of language groups, people groups and segments of societies that are still unreached.

With the insights gleaned from research and collaboration, Christians have the opportunity to keep billions of unreached people from a Christless eternity in our generation. Following the examples of Jesus' teaching through parables, primary oral learners who comprise two-thirds of the world can comprehend God's word. The thorough method that oral strategies provide can assist in preventing syncretism. Oral learners can understand at their heart level, within their culture, what it means to follow Jesus. They can be discipled, become leaders and plant churches. Let us therefore go forth embracing oral communicators as partners, together making disciples of all peoples to the glory of God!

an annotated resource list

IN KEEPING with our interest in assisting churches in ministry, we have listed below a number of resources that churches might use in making disciples of oral learners. This list is representative, not exhaustive. There are doubtless other fine resources not listed here.

In a listing as diverse as this, it is inevitable that some resources will be better suited to a given situation than others. Some of the resources below focus on ministry among unreached peoples having no literacy and no Scripture in their language, while other resources are intended for audiences with significant amounts of literacy. Some of the resources have been carefully tailored for a specific worldview; others have not been. Some resources are free of charge while others involve significant purchases. Some are intensely practical and simple; others are academic and technical in nature. We encourage pastors, churches, missionaries, researchers, and others to discern what resources would best suit their needs.

Resources on Orality, Bible Storying and Audio-Visual Bible Services and Products

Individual Resources

Charlton Heston Presents the Bible. 4 DVDs. GoodTimes DVD. (1993). *Shot on location in the Holy Land, this incredible production is more than great literature come to life--it is a walk through history itself. Connect with some of the most beautiful and relevant Bible stories. This is an educational and entertaining family activity, allowing the viewer to experience the power and drama set to rich musical scores. This Bible storytelling resource is in four parts: Genesis, Moses, Jesus, and the Passion.* www.hestonbible.com.

Communication Bridges to Oral Cultures—Master Trainer Series Manuals for Grass Roots Church Planters (80 pp.), Discipleship through Storytelling (68 pp.), Stories and Letters of the Apostles (34 pp.), accompanied by a 3-DVD set (3 hour video series) available in English, Spanish, French, Hindi, Mandarin, and Amharic (others in progress). *These resources are used for a four-day intensive training course for grass roots church planters. Approximately 75-100 training events are given each year in various parts of the world by Scriptures In Use and various partner agencies.*

Davis, Charlotte ed. Telling His Story in the Caribbean Basin: Chronological Bible Storying. *An electronic newsletter sharing the world of Chronological Bible Storying in the Caribbean and South/Central America. Subscribe free at* cdavi17@attglobal.net.

Evans, Steve. Communicating Christ in a Cross-Cultural Context: Developing Effective Media and Communication Strategies Leading to Church Planting Movements / The World of Orality. Workbook/ PowerPoint. (2004).

Evans, Steve. The World of Orality: Limited Edition is a 43-page mini workbook taken from the much larger Communicating Christ in a Cross-Cultural Context: Developing Effective Media and Communication Strategies Leading to Church Planting Movements. *It is a good introduction to the world of orality and the development of strategies to reach oral peoples. The accompanying PowerPoint is a general overview of orality and its impact on Christian work around the world. Free download at* http://www.communication-strategy.net/synapse/documents/Files_public.cfm?website=communi cation-strategy.net

The HOPE: The Story of God's Promise for All People. Mars Hill Productions.
Created in cooperation with motion picture producers and distributors around the world, The HOPE is a powerful dramatic overview of an incredible story–the Bible–a story many have called the greatest ever told. Designed for cultural adaptation and language translation, The HOPE is divided into 12 chapters and 36 events and is available in VHS or DVD format. For information go to http://www.mars-hill.org/media/the_hope_main/the_hope_set.htm.

My Place in HIStory. Study Course/Multi-Media. Lifeway Christian Resources. (1999).
A videotape and workbook church training course on how to use Chronological Bible Storying to share the gospel with family, friends and neighbours. https://www.lifeway.com/cgsp/english/catalog *(then do a resource search and indicate* My Place in HIStory*).*

Norwood, Johnny. Storying for Evangelism and Church Planting (Textbook and Teacher's Manual): For Training Christian Leaders to Teach Both Literate and Oral Oriented Learners How to Do Chronological Bible Storying in Antagonistic as Well as Sympathetic Settings. Chiang Mai, Thailand (2003).
A step-by-step manual on using pre-selected chronological Bible stories for personal evangelism. For information write jnorwood@ gsnconsultants.com.

*Tell the Story: A Primer on Chronological Bible Storying. Workbook/ Study Course. International Center for Excellence in Leadership, 2003.
Learn how to reach oral communicators effectively with the gospel using this workbook including CD. This workbook consists of 13 lessons, starting with the world of stories to using Chronological Bible Storying for church planting movement strategies. For information go to http://resources.imb.org/index.cfm/fa/prod/ProdID/1140.htm.

Terry J.O. ed. Bible Storying: God's Word Story by Story to Empower Every Person Oral or Literate for Witness and Discipling Their Own. *An electronic newsletter on Chronological Bible Storying worldwide. Subscribe free at* biblestorying@sbcglobal.net.

Terry J.O. ed. Journal of Bible Storying. *An electronic journal on the more academic and scholarly side of Chronological Bible Storying. Subscribe free at* biblestorying@sbcglobal.net.

Willis, Avery. Following Jesus: Making Disciples of Primary Oral Learners. Audio CDs. (2003). Progressive Vision. *Your answer to critical issues: 1) getting the gospel to all nations; 2) communicating with non-literates; 3) addressing syncretism problems; 4) making disciples of oral learners who comprise 70% of the world's population; 5) the next wave of missions advance. Designed to reach illiterates, functionally illiterates, semi-literates, storying cultures and many others who simply prefer a non-literate approach. Following Jesus consists of seven learning modules that frame this learning experience on audio CD! Designed for translation and cultural adaptation. For information go to* http://fjseries.org.

Organizations, Resources, Services, and Products

The Bible Storytelling Project

The Bible Storytelling Project uses Bible stories in chronological order for the purpose of evangelizing, teaching, preaching, planting new churches and training church leaders. Bible stories in chronological order give a panoramic view of the Bible and an overview of basic Bible doctrine. This project has numerous Bible storytelling resources, including *Storying the Bible: Tools for Bible Storytelling* by Jackson Day. Age-level curriculum is available in English, Spanish, and Portuguese. Contact jackday@pobox.com or http://biblestorytelling.org.

Deaf Church Planting Network

The "Deaf Sign-Bible" visual program is being developed in several sign languages. This includes video, DVD or CD recording accompanied by a set of story cards. The presentation utilizes a system of iconic symbols to aid in memorization and presentation of gospel truths. The presentations provide an overview of the Bible from creation to Christ the way of salvation, the basics of the Christian life, and strategies for church planting. This is an excellent evangelism, discipling, and church planting resource for the Deaf. Also, there are visual recordings of Bible messages in various signed languages. (These are a selection of short Bible stories or messages signed by native Deaf sign users). For more information and list of signed languages go to www.deafchurches.net.

Deaf Opportunity OutReach International (D.O.O.R.)

D.O.O.R. (Deaf Opportunity Out Reach International) uses Chronological Bible Storying in its three regional leadership-training centres: 1) Nairobi, Kenya, 2) San Jose, Costa Rica, and 3) Budapest, Hungary. They have trained 240 Deaf Christians from 44 countries. For more information go to www.DOORInternational.com.

Faith Comes By Hearing

FCBH has dramatized word-for-word recordings of the entire New Testament in 150 languages, with 50 more in process. They also have training on how to use these recordings to disciple oral people through the formation of Faith Comes By Hearing listening groups. There are 25 national recording teams in 12 Recording Service Centres located throughout the world that are trained to do dramatized recordings including music and sound effects with cutting edge portable digital recording and editing equipment. For more information visit www.fcbh.org.

Global Recordings Network/Gospel Recordings

Global Recordings Network has produced the following resources suitable for use with and by non- or minimally-literate people (oral communicators): *Gospel Messages* in over 5,500 languages. (These are usually a selection of short Bible stories or messages spoken by mother tongue speakers and sometimes incorporate indigenous music); the *Good News* audio-visual program available in over 900 languages (this includes a cassette or CD recording accompanied by a set of 40 pictures giving a brief overview of the Bible from creation to Christ the way of salvation and the basics of the Christian life); the *Look, Listen and Live* audio presentation (available in more than 300 languages, consisting of 8 cassettes with accompanying picture sets: parts 1-5 cover Old Testament stories and themes, parts 6 & 7 cover the four Gospels and part 8 covers the book Acts); *The Living Christ* audio-visual presentation (available in about 30 languages, with 120 loose leaf pictures and commentary on 2 cassettes – the pictures come with a printed script and a set of 20 short lessons for use as a teaching resource). All pictures are also available as black and white line drawings. GRN also offers hand-wind cassette players for use where there is no power and batteries are expensive or not available. For more information, prices and orders go to www.globalrecordings.net.

The God's Story Project

The 80-minute presentation, *God's Story: From Creation to Eternity*, presents the Bible from Genesis to Revelation. Throughout the Old and New Testaments, this panorama of the Scriptures highlights God's plan to rescue fallen mankind. For evangelism and discipling. Available in video, VCD (video CD), audiocassette, audio CD. In total there are over 200 language translations of *God's Story* either finished, in various stages of negotiation or in script translation. This does not include the over one thousand languages that have also been requested. "Our desire is to partner with national Christians, willing to share the workload, to produce a tool for them to use for evangelism and discipleship in their country." TGSP features a village-size backpack containing a VCD player, *God's Story* on Video CD (VCD), a solar panel and a battery power source. These items enable an evangelist to deliver the gospel via *God's Story* to homes and gatherings in remote areas where there is no electricity! Optional PA with wireless mic projects sound clearly to 500 feet. Script, discussion guide and radio script are also available. For information go to www.Gods-Story.org or www.biblevideo.org.

The JESUS Film Project

The *JESUS Film* Project distributes the film "JESUS," a two-hour docudrama about the life of Christ based on the Gospel of Luke. The film has been seen in every country of the world and translated into over 870 languages since its initial release in 1979. The goal is to reach every nation, tribe, people, and tongue, helping them see and hear the story of Jesus in a language they can understand. Through use by The JESUS Film Project, and more than 1,500 Christian agencies, this powerful film has had more than 5 billion viewings worldwide since 1979. As a result, more than 197 million people have indicated decisions to accept Christ as their personal Savior and Lord. The *JESUS* film is available in video, VCD, and DVD formats, as well as in a special children's edition and audio-radio format. Other resources are available as well. Go to http://www.jesusfilmstore.com/Merchant2/merchant.mvc?Screen=SFNT.

MegaVoice

MegaVoice: *The Word in Hand.* "Break the Silence...Finish the Task." A unique application in voice storage and retrieval, designed to dramatically accelerate dissemination of vital information, including God's Word, Chronological Bible Stories, etc. The *MegaVoice Ambassador* is a palm-sized, self-contained digital audio player designed to store up to 160 hours of material and has an internal solar panel for rechargeable batteries. The *MegaVoice Messenger* is a smaller unit, designed to store up to one hour of material, and has been known as the "Talking Tract." For information visit www.megavoice.com or write info@megavoice.com.

Mission Education Books (MEB)

Mission Education Books is located in Chennai, India and has a wealth of resources on orality, church planting, and Bible storying. They have *Discipleship through Storytelling, Gospel Communication Bridges for Non-Literates* by S. D. Ponraj and Jim Bowman, *Communication Bridges to Oral Cultures II,* and more. Many titles are in languages of India. For information go to http://www.missionbooks.net/pubtraining.htm.

New Tribes Mission

EE-TAOW!; EE-TAOW! The Next Chapter; and *Now We See Clearly.* Videos/DVDs. New Tribes Mission. Discover the success of chronological presentations of God's Word for effective church planting, discipleship, and correction of syncretism. Go to http://www.ntmbooks.com/index.cfm?fuseaction=catalog.shop&shop Action=listCategory&categoryID=5&sr=1. In addition to numerous other resources, NTM offers *Bible Teaching Pictures* on CD. Both in colour and B&W line drawings, this CD contains 105 Bible story pictures to be used in chronological narrative presentations of God's Word. For information go to http://www.ntmbooks.com/index.cfm?fuseaction=catalog.shop&shopA ction=itemDetail&catalogID=116&categoryid=1&myInventoryID=33

The Radio Bible Project

The Radio Bible Project is a global partnership between Hosanna/Faith Comes By Hearing, the International Bible Society, Trans World Radio, and the United Bible Societies formed to bring the Word of God to oral societies. The Radio Bible consists of 365 fifteen-minute broadcasts of stories from the Old and New Testaments. These programs allow both literate and oral communicators the opportunity to hear the Bible in an engaging fashion. While the core of the Radio Bible is a dramatized Scripture presentation, it also includes background and engagement material so listeners can understand and apply the Scriptural stories to their daily lives. Find more information about this project at www.theradiobible.org.

Scriptures In Use

Scriptures In Use specializes in training grass roots church planters to communicate the Oral Bible, guiding and mentoring each church planter to develop a grass roots church planting ministry through simple Bible storytelling and other traditional oral communication media. http://www.siutraining.org. SIU offers *Communication Bridges to Oral Cultures* training course that instills a love for the Scriptures in the mother tongue through a systematic chronological Bible storytelling approach. This 4-day, intensive training teaches the fundamentals of evangelism and discipleship for local leaders or trainers working among non-literate or traditionally oral people groups, and provides: 1) emphasis on church planting through chronological Scripture storytelling in the cultural context of the people group; 2) practical training in effective Scripture storytelling methods; and 3) exploration of stories, adaptations of Scripture in song, dramatization of the parables, audio/video for effective communication to traditional oral cultures. An excellent overview of and tool for the training is *The Ancient Path: Church Planting for Oral Cultures.* DVDs. (2004). Scriptures In Use/Progressive Vision. For more information go to www.siutraining.org/resources.htm.

Vernacular Media Services

VMS brings the Word to the world in a culturally relevant way. "Vernacular" means the local language or mother tongue. "Media" is the path used to bring a message. Vernacular media specialists help Wycliffe Bible translators and national translators use media tools that are culturally appropriate. Scripture may be presented in the local language on video or audiocassette, or in radio programs, dance, or drama. These tools help establish a bridge for oral cultures to understand the Word of God. VMS asks: "What will help to make Scripture a part of these people's lives?" Media options are varied: audio and videocassettes, filmstrips, radio and television, live drama, puppets, and flipcharts. For more information go to http://www.jaars.org/vern.shtml.

Pictures and Related Visual Resources

Bible Pictures. Hong Kong: Hong Kong Baptist Press. A set of 40 traditional colour pictures from Noah to Shadrach, Meshach, and Abednego in the Old Testament, 17 on the life and ministry of Jesus, and 7 on Acts. Pictures are 12x17 inches on durable card stock.

Biblical Wall-Posters. National Biblical Catechetical and Liturgical Centre, Bangalore, India. Large bright colour Indian contextualized biblical posters covering creation to the restoration of Israel in 51 pictures and from the annunciation to Elizabeth to a new heaven and new earth in Revelation for a total of 140 pictures.

Colour It Tell It Bible Stories; Book One: Creation to Moses. Manila: Church Strengthening Ministry, 1992. Projected as a series of five story coloring books for use with children using line drawings taken from "Telling the Story..." color picture set. When completed the series will contain 103 Bible stories suitable for reading to children, to use in family devotions, or for church-centered Bible study or Sunday school. (Book Two: *Moses to Roman Rule*; Book Three: *The Birth of Jesus to the Transfiguration*; Book Four: *Jesus and the Children to the Ascension*; and Book Five: *the Acts of the Apostles.*) http://csm-publishing.net.

Dawson, David L. *A Visual Survey of the Bible.* Greenville, TX, 1982. The Bible's message illustrated in a fifteen foot color chart showing the panoramic story of redemption from creation to the return of Christ. Also available in Chinese, Korean, Spanish and other languages. The chart is also available as a black and white line drawing in which local languages could be drawn in and coloured. Accompanying text and choice of end times panels according to theological preference. 4400 Moulton Street, Suite D. Greenville, TX (USA) 75401. Tel 903-455-3782.

Farris, Mary Lou. *The Adam & Eve Family Tree.* Norman, OK. A helpful colour chart showing the genealogy of Jesus from Adam and Eve. It lists the family lines of the Old Testament along with the names of wives and offspring. It is helpful for sorting out the patriarchal and royal family genealogies. http://members.aol.com/tmcorner2/a-e_ft.htm.

Good News audiovisual - A set of 40 pictures, available in large (flipchart), medium and small (pocket size) formats, accompanied by a recorded 'commentary'. The story-based programme provides a brief overview of the Bible and then some basic teaching on getting right with God and living as a follower of Jesus. The recorded commentary is available in more than 900 languages. http://globalrecordings.net/au/prod-gn.html.

Life of Jesus Mafa. Versailles, France. Highly contextualized African teaching pictures with Jesus and all story characters portrayed as African Blacks in typical African village settings. Sixty colour pictures from the Annunciation to Pentecost. http://www.jesusmafa.com/anglais/accueil.htm.

Line Drawings for Bible Stories Asian Style. Bangkok: New Tribes Mission. Black and white line drawings lightly contextualized for Southeast Asians in 11x16 inch size supplied as photocopies. A total of 389 pictures divided into 46 "sets" of pictures consisting of 38 Pre-Bible pictures, 193 Old Testament pictures and 158 New Testament pictures. Suggested guide for colouring the pictures locally.

The Living Christ audiovisual–A set of 120 loose leaf, A4 size pictures based on the life of Christ with accompanying recorded commentary, printed script and set of short lesson scripts indicating which pictures to use for the lesson. The recorded commentary is available in about 30 languages. http://globalrecordings.net/au/prod-tlc.html.

Look, Listen & Live Bible Pictures and Scripts. Global Recordings Network, Inc. (Australia) An eight-part set of colour Bible pictures (2 formats available: flipcharts [17x13 inches] and picture booklets [5.5x8.5 inches] chronologically arranged with recorded story commentaries. The recorded commentaries are available in more than 200 languages. The first five parts cover Old Testament material while parts 6-8 are based on the Gospels and book of Acts. Printed scripts are available in several languages. The scripts are simple story presentations with Scripture base indicated. Each picture set contains four or five stories with multiple pictures for each story. 24 pictures in each flipchart or booklet. Flip charts are spiral bound at the top; booklets are stapled. http://globalrecordings.net/au/prod-lll.html.

Lukens, Betty. *The Bible in Felt.* A three-year cycle of presenting the Bible story chronologically through use of flannel graph pictures. Available in two sizes--classroom size (16x24 inches) and auditorium size (32x48 inches). May be used in place of flat pictures to illustrate, build, or tell the Bible story. Teacher's manual does not contain the stories but suggests background scenes and flannel graph figures to use for each Bible story passage. www.bettylukens.com.

Telling the Story. 105 Picture Set. Manila: Church Strengthening Ministry. A set of 105 individual 17x13 inch colour pictures (103 pictures and 2 maps) jointly developed by Philippine Baptist Mission and New Tribes Mission for use in chronological approaches to teaching. The pictures follow a chronological order and are presented with limited background detail and minimal perspective for use with those of limited visual literacy. Also available in 8.5x11 inch line drawings suitable for photocopy and colouring by local users. http://csm-publishing.net.

Web-Based Resources

http://www.augusthouse.com: August House is an award-winning publisher of children's books, folktale anthologies for all ages and stories for classroom use in book and audio formats. Their books are used in literacy and Title I programs to build language, critical thinking and writing skills even as they entertain. Parents and teachers use August House books, tapes, and CDs in reading comprehension and diversity study, character education, and cross-curriculum lesson plans. Scout leaders and summer camps use their scary story books, world folktales, and trickster tales around the campfire. Sunday School educators use their tales of wisdom and justice as discussion openers. Storytellers use August House storytelling skills handbooks for story resources, for ethnic sourcing, and to prepare for telling stories or public speaking.

http://biblestorytelling.org: The Bible Storytelling Project uses Bible stories in chronological order for the purpose of evangelizing, teaching, preaching, planting new churches, and training church leaders. Bible stories in chronological order give a panoramic view of the Bible and an overview of basic Bible doctrine. This site contains numerous Bible storytelling resources.

http://www.christianstorytelling.com: Their goal is to network Christian storytellers and nurture storytelling in the Christian community. They want to be a resource for churches and Christian organizations. Believing that God has put into each individual a love for hearing a good story, this web site and its creator, John Walsh, encourage storytelling as a powerful way to communicate God's grace to others. John Walsh is dedicated to offering a free story each month, resources for developing storytelling skills, and a growing list of Christian storytellers across the U. S. who are available to perform and to train others in storytelling. Storytelling curriculum and Christian school resources are also available.

http://chronologicalbiblestorying.com: The official Chronological Bible Storying website. Contains training manuals, story sets, advice, research reports, articles, readers, PowerPoint presentations and a number of other helpful training resources.

http://www.communication-strategy.net: The Communication Strategy Network carries a number of articles on Chronological Bible Storying, orality and the use of media for effective church planting strategies; has a number of free downloads; and uses e-newsletter--free by subscription.

http://www.OneStory.org: OneStory was founded by four mission-sending organizations: Campus Crusade, International Mission Board, Wycliffe International and YWAM. The web site provides information on Quest, Venture, and Journey options. The main goal of OneStory is to provide God's Word for oral learners without Bibles and who are lost.

http://www.mediastrategy.org: Mediastrategy is produced by media strategist Dan Henrich of Liberty University; stays current through active blog.

www.nobs.org: The Network of Biblical Storytellers (NOBS) is an international organization whose mission is to communicate the sacred stories of the biblical tradition. It was formed nearly twenty years ago by people searching for ways to experience and hear anew the word of God as narrative. NOBS develops resources for telling biblical stories through audio, video and computer technologies as well as telling them face-to-face. Members come from the USA, Canada, Australia, Europe, Japan, Singapore, South Africa, the Philippines, and New Zealand. NOBS sponsors the Journal of Biblical Storytelling (http://www.nobs.org/journal.htm). P.O. Box 413, Brookville, OH 45309 (USA). TEL 937-833-4141 or 1-800-355-NOBS (from USA); FAX 937-833-5603; nobsint@nobs.org.

http://internationaloralitynetwork.com: A network founded by nine missions agencies. The International Orality Network has conducted consultations and training workshops for learners and experienced storyers. Member organizations include Campus Crusade, International Mission Board (SBC), Wycliffe International, TWR, the JESUS Film Project, Faith Comes By Hearing, Scriptures In Use, The Seed Company, and the God's Story Project.

http://www.stevedenning.com: Steve Denning consults and gives workshops and keynote presentations on topics that include: leadership, innovation, organizational storytelling, business storytelling, springboard storytelling, knowledge management, branding, marketing, values, communication, communities of practice, business performance, collective intelligence, tacit knowledge, business collaboration, knowledge, learning, community, performance improvement, visionary leadership, social potential, institutional community building and internal communications. The site has many storytelling resources.

http://www.storytellingcenter.net: U.S.-based International Storytelling Centre. Inspired by an international renaissance of storytelling, people around the world are turning to the ancient tradition of storytelling to produce positive change in our world. The International Storytelling Center-to further infuse storytelling into the mainstream of our society - is building on its 30-year history to promote the power of storytelling and its creative applications to build a better world. This site is abundant in storytelling resources and activities.

http://www.storynet.org: U.S.-based National Storytellers Network. "Bringing together and nurturing individuals and organizations that use the power of storytelling in all its forms." In addition to numerous resources, NSN features *Storytellers Magazine* and *Storytelling World*. *Storytelling Magazine* is published bimonthly by National Storytelling Network and is available at no charge to NSN Members. Subscriptions only to *Storytelling Magazine* are not available. Single copies, however, may be purchased for $6.50 ($4.95 per issue plus shipping) to U.S. addresses. Storytelling World magazine is now offered as a membership benefit for the National Storytelling Network and is also available via subscription.

http://strategyleader.org: Orville Boyd Jenkins' virtual research centre offers a wide variety of research tools and information about key issues like worldview definition and study, plus people group and ethnicity issues. It is a great resource for learning about the underlying issues of serving oral peoples in a post-literate world. Available resources include up-to-date PowerPoint presentations.

http://www.kn.pacbell.com/wired/fil/pages/liststorytelvi.html: Storytelling—Tales to Tell bills itself as "an internet hotlist on storytelling" and lists dozens of storytelling links.

Bible Software Useful in Story Crafting

BibleWorks 6.0 - Computer software contains 93 Bible translations in 29 languages, 12 original language texts with 7 morphology databases, 6 Greek lexicons and dictionaries, 4 Hebrew lexicons and dictionaries, plus 18 practical reference works! While other programs are m e r e l y loose collections of books, BibleWorks tightly integrates its databases with the most   powerful morphology and analysis tools. Considered a high-end Bible research package competitively   priced, BibleWorks has a quality database, permits programming, search capabilities and customer support. Cost: $299.95. Order info online at www.bibleworks. com or www.discountbible.com (which includes free shipping and a free software package worth $29.95).

Bible Navigator - Computer software offers powerful search features, fast cross-referencing, and an integrated word processor. This CD-ROM product includes the complete new Holman Christian Standard Bible and a library of reference works. Personalization features maximize its value for reading and study while Internet-enhancements extend your learning. $19.97. Order online at http://www.lifewaystores.com.

iLumina - (Gold edition) is the world's first digitally animated Bible and encyclopedia suite. Carries the full text of the Bible in the New Living Translation and King James Version. The package also includes commentary on every verse and a complete illustrated encyclopedia. iLumina Gold provides computer animations guided virtual tours of the Holy Land, 20,000 notes and commentaries, and 42 documentary videos on the life of Jesus. Compatible with Windows or Mac OS X. Cost: $89.99 at http://www.iLumina.com or www.Amazon.com.

Logos Bible Series X - Computer software can make your personal Bible study easier and more productive by giving you access to more content and by acting as an automated "research assistant" that searches, organizes and presents that content in ways that accelerate your study and draw you deeper into the word. Series X lets you have different levels of software - Christian Home Library ($150), Bible Study Library ($250), Pastor's Library ($300), Original Languages Library ($400) and Scholar's Libraries ($600) and Silver Edition ($1,000). The Silver edition contains everything in the X Series; each series builds on the next. (Prices rounded.) The Bible Study Library, for instance, has 115 Bibles, a Greek and Hebrew dictionary, several commentaries, and references that normally cost $2,500 in purchased volumes for $249.95. Order online at http://www.logos.com.

bibliography

ORALITY is a multi-faceted phenomenon that has drawn the attention of writers in many disciplines. Historians, biblical scholars, linguists, psychologists, educators, students of folk tales, communications experts, business consultants, professional storytellers, missionaries, and leaders of emerging churches: all of these and more have written about the phenomenon we refer to as orality. Consequently this bibliography includes a wide variety of books, some of which do not use the term "orality" and many of which have no concern for Christian ministry. Members of the Lausanne special interest group have found useful information in each of them, however. If nothing else, this wide array of books confirms the central role that orality plays in the contemporary world, especially in communication and the shaping of values. Thus far only a few authors have sought to draw on this wide array of scholarship to improve our effectiveness in making disciples of oral learners. But work is in progress that will hopefully meet that need in the years to come.

Books marked with an asterisk (*) in the list below are recommended for Bible college and theological libraries.

Books

Anderson, John R. <u>Cognitive Psychology and Its Implications</u>. 4th ed. New York: W. H. Freeman, 1995. *In Anderson's discussion of cognitive schemata and worldview, one can understand the importance of story repetition in the avoidance of error.*

Baddeley, A. D. <u>The Psychology of Memory</u>. New York: Basic Books, 1976.

Baush, William J. <u>Storytelling: Imagination and Faith</u>. Mystic, CT: Twenty-Third Publications, 1984. *Bausch refers to a wealth and breadth of stories to capture and pass on from one generation to another the wisdom, imagination, and faith of a people. This is a book of stories as well as a book about storytelling.*

Baush, William J. <u>Storytelling the Word: Homilies & How to Write Them</u>. Mystic-Connecticut: Twenty-Third Publications, 1996. *This book contains 42 homilies and 130 stories used to instruct the reader in the art of storytelling combined with narrative preaching. An appendix correlates the homilies to specific liturgical seasons and a lectionary of readings.*

Bilmes, Jack and Stephen T. Boggs. "Language and Communication: The Foundations of Culture." In <u>Perspectives on Cross-Cultural Psychology</u>, ed. Anthony Marsella, Roland Tharp, and Thomas Ciborowski, 47-76. New York: Academic Press, 1979. *The authors identify the reality of culture as systems of knowledge in persons' minds.*

Birch, Carol L. and Melissa A. Heckler, eds. <u>*Who Says?: Essays on Pivotal Issues in Contemporary Storytelling.*</u> Little Rock: August House, 1990. *The editors provide ten essays by various writers addressing critical issues in an increasingly potent movement–that of storytelling. They assert that the movement is young and there is no common vocabulary for discussion.*

*Boomershine, Thomas E. <u>Story Journey. An Invitation to the Gospel as Storytelling</u>. Nashville: Abingdon Press, 1988. *Using illustrations from the Gospel of Mark, Boomershine makes an excellent case for telling the gospel as stories. He gives practical instruction on learning, remembering, and telling biblical stories for a variety of ministry purposes.*

Breech, James. <u>Jesus and Postmodernism</u>. Minneapolis: Augsburg Fortress, 1989. *James Breech traces Jesus the storyteller. He looks to the parables of Jesus and their divine uniqueness, their narrative integrity, their truth, and their ethical stance. In this work, the author engages two movements in contemporary theology: postmodernism and narrative theology.*

Campbell, Joseph. The Hero with a Thousand Faces. New York: Pantheon, 1949. *From the well-known interpreter on mythology, this classic study traces the story of the hero's journey and transformation through virtually all the mythologies of the world, revealing the one archetypal hero in them all.*

Carruthers, Mary J. The Book of Memory: A Study of Memory in Medieval Culture. New York: Cambridge University Press, 1992.

Cate, Mary Ann and Karol Downey. From Fear to Faith: Muslim Women and Christian Women. Pasadena, CA: William Carey Library, 2003. *This is a compendium of messages presented at a conference on reaching Muslim women. The focus is on Muslim women and strategies to lead them to a mature, reproducing faith in Christ. Of particular interest would be the chapters on the Muslim woman's view of God and why Muslim women come to Christ. There is also a chapter describing the use of Chronological Bible Storying as one method of outreach.*

Chomsky, Noam. Language and Mind. New York: Oxford University Press, 1968.

Cipolla, Carlo M. Literacy and Development in the West. New York: Penguin Books. 1969. *This traces the historic emergence of languages, reading, writing, and thus literacy from at least the Classic Greek era to the 1900s. It assists the reader in understanding the historic development of literacy, which is only recent and not that pervasive, even by A.D. 2000.*

Clanchy, M. T. From Memory to Written Record: England, 1066-1307. London: Edward Arnold, 1979.

Cole, Michael, John Gay, Joseph A. Glick, and Donald W. Sharp. The Cultural Context of Learning and Thinking. New York: Basic Books, 1971. *An interesting report of cognitive experiments conducted with non-literates in Africa.*

Cole, Michael and Sylvia Scribner. Culture and Thought. New York: Wiley, 1974. *Two influential researchers explore the influence of culture on habitual ways of thinking.*

Connelly, Bridget. Arab Folk Epic and Identity. Berkeley, CA: University of California Press, 1986.

D'Andrade, Roy. "Culture and Human Cognition." In Cultural Psychology: Essays on Comparative Human Development, ed. James W. Stigler, Richard A. Shweder, and Gilbert Herdt, 65-129. New York: Cambridge University Press, 1990. *D'Andrade discusses the concept of cognitive schemata and the link between culture, language, and cognition.*

Davidson, J. A. Literature and Literacy in Ancient Greece. Phoenix 14 (1962), nos. 3-4.

Davis, Donald. Writing as a Second Language: From Experience to Story to Prose. Little Rock: August House, 2000. *Davis addresses the issue of language arts in schools, where focus is on reading and writing instead of nourishing the whole oral and kinesthetic realm, that of spoken language. He argues that talking and writing are not to be mutually exclusive in language development and lays out a method to address the issue.*

Egan, Kieran. Teaching as Storytelling: An Alternative Approach to Teaching and Curriculum in the Elementary School. Chicago: University of Chicago Press, 1986. *Egan argues the case for storytelling from an educational perspective, contending that stories are a very sophisticated way of developing both intellect and imagination. He gives special attention to using storytelling across the curriculum.*

*Enyart, David A. Creative Anticipation: Narrative Sermon Designs for Telling the Story. N. p.: Xlibris, 2002. *Enyart introduces preachers to a variety of ways to preach biblical narratives.*

Finnegan, Ruth. Limba Stories and Storytelling. London: Oxford University Press, 1967. *This is the best book for looking inside a specific socio-linguistic culture in West Africa to see the issues of orality and literacy as they existed within these people. It is a very scholarly, but practical and easy to read book. An influential study of storytelling practices and their impact in the Limba culture of West Africa, it is widely quoted within the discipline.*

Freidman, Thomas L. The Lexus and the Olive Tree: Understanding Globalization. New York: Anchor Books, 1999. *This book offers an engrossing look at the international system that is transforming the world today–globalization. With vivid stories drawn from his extensive travels, Friedman dramatizes the conflict between "the Lexus and the olive tree"--the tension between the globalization system and the ancient forces of culture, geography, tradition, and community.*

Gerhardsson, Birger, Memory and Manuscript: Oral Tradition and Written Transmission in Rabbinic Judaism and Early Christianity. Copenhagen: Gleerup and Lund, 1961. *Gerhardsson deals with the respective roles of memory and manuscripts, orality and literacy from the Abrahamic era to well beyond the New Testament era. He gives a detailed, technical description of the careful, conscious process of transmitting religious instruction during the biblical period and beyond. Frequently dismissed but never refuted, Gerhardsson persisted in setting forth his views and defending his arguments about the relationship of the text to oral and literate religious leaders.* Tradition and Transmission in Early Christianity, *published in 1964, clarified his views and replied to critics. In 1998 Eerdmans released a single volume combining* Memory and Manuscript *with* Tradition and Transmission *and adding new material, including an apology from one of Gerhardsson's early critics, who admits that he and others did not read Gerhardsson's work carefully and thus misrepresented him.*

Gibbs, Eddie and Ian Coffey. Church Next: Quantum Changes in Christian Ministry. Downers Grove, IL: Inter Varsity Press, 2001. *The authors of this book identify some of the major storm centers through which the church must navigate, not in order to return to a previously more tranquil world, but to enter an entirely new one. The book looks at mission, church structures, developing new leaders and mentoring, worship, spirituality and evangelism, and asks how ministry must change in order to serve a new generation of Christians.*

Goodwin, Frank J. A Harmony of the Life of St. Paul. Baker Book House, 1960. *A generally helpful volume for those preparing integrated Acts-Epistles story lessons for advanced tracks of chronological method after the basic evangelism and review tracks. The author integrates the missionary journeys of Paul with the letters written to the churches. May be a bit difficult for the average user, but could be helpful for those preparing lessons for local area use.*

Goody, Jack. Literacy in Traditional Societies. Cambridge: Cambridge University Press, 1968.

Goody, Jack. The Domestication of the Savage Mind. Cambridge: Cambridge University Press, 1977. *This is an influential book describing the effects of literacy on non-literate societies and their patterns of thinking.*

Graff, Harvey J. The Legacies of Literacy: Continuities and Contradictions in Western Culture and Society. Bloomington: Indiana University Press, 1987. *Graff's work is an outstanding history of the development of literacy in the West and its influence on western culture.*

Graham, William A. Beyond the Written Word: Oral Aspects of Scripture in he History of Religion. Cambridge: Cambridge UP, 1987. *Graham compares orality and literacy in major religions having both written and oral traditions.*

Haaland, Ane. Pretesting Communication Materials. Burma: UNICEF Publications, 1984. *This source is helpful in determining whether communication materials will be received and correctly perceived among a specific audience.*

Harold, Innis. The Bias of Communication. Toronto: University of Toronto Press, 1951.

Harris, Joseph, ed. The Ballad and Oral Literature. Cambridge, MA: Harvard University Press, 1991.

Harris, William V. Ancient Literacy. Cambridge, MA: Harvard University Press, 1989. *A respected historian explores the nature and extent of literacy in the ancient world. This is a standard work on this topic.*

Havelock, Eric. The Greek Concept of Justice from Its Shadow in Homer to Its Substance in Plato. Cambridge, MA: Harvard University Press. 1978.

Havelock, Eric. The Muse Learns to Write: Reflections on Orality and Literacy from Antiquity to the Present. New Haven: CT: Yale University Press, 1988. *A leading scholar in the historical development of literacy, Havelock presents here the fruit of a lifetime of study on this issue.*

Jaffee, Martin S. Torah in the Mouth: Writing and Oral Tradition in Palestinian Judaism 200 BCE-400 CE. Oxford: Oxford University Press, 2001. *Jaffee explores the relationship between the written and oral sources in Palestinian Judaism during the era that included the development of Christianity.*

Jensen, Richard A. Thinking in Story: Preaching in a Post-literate Age. Lima, Ohio: CSS Publishing, 1993. *Poised on the boundary between the print and electronic era, the contemporary church needs to rethink preaching. To this end Jensen offers a strategy for effective communication in this electronic era. Due to present-day media saturation, the author calls for a shift in approaches to gospel proclamation. Jensen argues that trends in western culture make it necessary for Christians to begin thinking in stories and preaching using biblical narratives. He tells how to do this and gives sample sermons.*

*Jousse, Marcel. Le Style Oral Rhythmique et Mnemotechnique Chez les Verbo-moteurs Paris: G. Beauchesne, 1925; ET, *The Oral Style.* Translated by Edgard Sienaert and Richard Whitaker. New York. Garland, 1990. *One of the early attempts by scholars to describe in detail the methods used by oral communicators.*

Kelber, Werner. The Oral and Written Gospel: The Hermeneutics of Speaking and Writing in the Synoptic Tradition. Mark. Paul and Q. Philadelphia: Fortress Press, 1983. *Kelber discusses the interplay of oral and written sources with respect to the gospel accounts.*

*Klem, Herbert V. Oral Communication of the Scripture. Pasadena: William Carey Library, 1982. *The author builds his case for oral communication of the Bible based upon the prevailing literacy situation and oral communication preferences of the African people, and of the situation in Palestine during Jesus' day. He also covers aspects of oral art forms. He includes important concepts for those involved in literacy work as well as evangelizing among illiterates. This study is focused primarily on West Africa.*

Levy-Strauss, Claude. La Pensee Sauvage. Paris: Plon, 1962; ET, The Savage Mind. Chicago: University of Chicago Press, 1966.

Lipman, Doug. Improving Your Storytelling: Beyond the Basics for All Who Tell Stories in Work or Play. Little Rock: August House, 1999. *This book takes the reader beyond the first, almost natural, steps of storytelling into the world of its more formal contexts. Instead of rules to follow, Lipman provides a series of frameworks that encourages "thinking on your feet." Part of the book looks at the transfer of imagery in a medium that is simultaneously visual, auditory, and kinesthetic.*

Lord, Albert B. The Singer of Tales. Harvard Studies in Comparative Literature, vol. 24. 2d ed. Cambridge, MA: Harvard University Press, 2000. *This edition of Lord's classic work on Yugoslavian epic poets includes a CD with audio and video recordings of the performances that are the focus of his research. This research, done by Milman Parry and his student, Albert Lord, enabled them to describe how illiterate poets were able to compose monumental epics like the* Iliad *and* Odyssey. *This volume established conclusively that oral cultures are capable of producing lengthy, complicated, and beautiful oral art forms without the use of print and reproduce them with accuracy over long periods of time.*

Love, Fran and Jeleta Eckheart. Ministry to Muslim Women: Longing to Call Them Sisters. Pasadena, CA: William Carey Library, 2000. *This is a compendium of messages presented at a conference on evangelism of Muslim women. It has an extensive section on worldview with several different articles on this subject. The book includes strategies for reaching Muslim women.*

Luria, A. R. Cognitive Development: Its Cultural and Social Foundations. Edited by Michael Cole. Translated by Martin Lopez-Morillas and Lynn Solotaroff. Cambridge, MA, and London: Harvard University Press, 1976. *Luria's research into peasant life in central Asia had pronounced impact on Walter Ong and the development of later understandings of the impact of literacy on oral peoples, especially in their cognitive development.*

Luria, A. R. The Mind of a Mnemonist. Translated by Lynn Solotaroff. New York: Basic Books, 1968. *Luria gives a description of a remarkable journalist who remembered everything that had ever happened to him and explores what that phenomenon reveals about the human memory.*

MacDonald, Margaret Read. The Storyteller's Start-Up Book: Finding, Learning, Performing and Using Folktales. Little Rock: August House, 1993. *The author believes that every community needs storytellers, actively sharing stories in the classroom, library, recreation centre, and boardroom. MacDonald's step-by-step process is an encouragement for beginners to have confidence in storytelling.*

*McLuhan, Marshall. The Gutenberg Galaxy: The Making of Typographic Man. Toronto: University of Toronto Press, 1962. *McLuhan was a well-known communications, linguistics, and media specialist. This classic work gave the world the concept of the "global village." It looks back at what the printing revolution did to the world and reflects on what the electronic age will do--creating a totally different world that is almost inconceivable even today. This is an excellent companion book to read along with Cipolla's work.*

Maguire, Jack. The Power of Personal Storytelling: Spinning Tales to Connect With Others. New York: Putnam, 1988. *Maguire explains how to mine stories buried deep within memory to communicate more effectively, enhance personal and professional relationships, and understand oneself in order to better understand others. Step by step he illustrates how to shape and express true-life stories.*

Malinowski, Bronislaw The Meaning of Meaning: A Study of the Influence of Language upon Thought and of the Science of Symbolism. New York: Harcourt, Brace; London: Kegan Paul, Trench, Trubner, 1923.

*Mathewson, Steven D. The Art of Preaching Old Testament Narrative. Grand Rapids, MI: Baker Academic, 2002.

Miller, Joseph C. The African Past Speaks: Essays on Oral Tradition and History. London: Dawson; Hamden, CT.: Archon, 1980.

Miller, Ted, ed. The Story. Carol Stream, IL: Tyndale House, 1986. *The Story is an edited version of the Living Bible which presents the Bible story as a continuing and integrated narrative in which individual stories are identified. This volume is of great help in learning how to present the Bible narratively, especially during the time of the kings and prophets and later in the Acts and epistles. While some of the better-known stories are somewhat abridged, enough of the story detail is retained to show the work and purpose of God in carrying out His work of redemption.*

Mooney, Bill and David Holt. The Storyteller's Guide. Little Rock, AR: August House, 1996. *Mooney and Holt have collected, edited, and written practical advice from a wide array of professional storytellers. They address issues such as how to create stories from printed texts, how to memorize and rehearse a story, the use of performance techniques, dealing with stage fright, avoiding frequent mistakes made by beginning storytellers, and using stories in a variety of situations.*

Olson, David R. "The Languages of Instruction: The Literate Bias of Schooling." In Schooling and the Acquisition of Knowledge, ed. Richard C. Anderson, Rand J. Spiro, and William E. Montague, 65-98. New York: John Wiley & Sons, 1977. *Olson discusses how humans acquire knowledge.*

*Ong, Walter J. Orality and Literacy: The Technologizing of the Word. London and New York: Routledge, 1982. *This is a technical treatise covering the modern discovery of primary oral cultures, some psychodynamics of orality, and oral memory, the story line, and characterization. It is more suitable for those interested in a deeper study of orality and its role in communication. This is the basic scholarly work in the field to date. No other work has superseded it. Ong takes account of all the major scholarly investigations through 1980.*

Postman, Leo and Geoffrey Keppel, eds. Verbal Learning and Memory. Baltimore, Penguin, 1969.

Rosenberg, Bruce A. Can These Bones Live? The Art of the American Folk Preacher. Rev. ed. Urbana: University of Illinois Press, 1988. *Rosenberg's study focuses on folk preachers, many of them rural pastors, whose sermonic style is influenced by oral traditions of preaching rather than formal academic instruction in preaching. His extensive interviews with the preachers offer insight into oral methods of composition and delivery.*

Rubin, David. Memory in Oral Traditions: The Cognitive Psychology of Epic, Ballads, and Counting-Out Rhymes. New York: Oxford University Press, 1995.

Rumelhart, David E. "Schemata: The Building Blocks of Cognition. In Theoretical Issues in Reading Comprehension, ed. Rand J. Spiro, Bertram C. Bruce, and William F. Brewer, 33-58. Hillsdale, New Jersey: Lawrence Erlbaum, 1980. *This chapter includes a discussion of cognitive schemata and their importance in information processing and memory recall.*

Sample, Tex. Ministry in an Oral Culture: Living with Will Rogers, Uncle Remus, and Minnie Pearl. Louisville, KY: John Knox Press, 1994. *Sample offers a popularly-written description of traditional oral culture in the United States and its implications for congregational decision making and ethics. This book is very helpful for understanding the unique dynamics of oral-culture churches, whether rural or urban.*

Scribner, Sylvia, and Michael Cole. The Psychology of Literacy. Cambridge, MA: Harvard University Press, 1981.

Simons, Annette. The Story Factor: Inspiration, Influence and Persuasion through the Art of Storytelling. Cambridge: Perseus, 2001.

Spradley, J. P. Culture and Cognition: Rule, Maps and Plans. San Francisco: Chandler, 1972. *A helpful source for envisioning the various aspects of a culture as one seeks to investigate and understand that culture.*

*Steffen, Tom A. Reconnecting God's Story to Ministry: Crosscultural Storytelling at Home and Abroad. La Habra, CA: Center for Organizational & Ministry Development, 1996. *Steffen draws on a wide array of sources to build a concise but strong case for using Bible storytelling in ministry. He includes a good bibliography of missions-related books and articles related to the topic.*

Tannen, Deborah, ed. Spoken and Written Language: Exploring Orality and Literacy. Advances in Discourse Processes, vol. 9. Norwood, NJ: Ablex, 1982. *This is a collection of articles on oral and written language including references to Japanese, Chinese, and Javanese, the comparison of comprehension and memory vs. written materials, and literary complexity in everyday storytelling.*

Tannen, Deborah. The Pear Stories: Cultural, Cognitive, and Linguistic Aspects of Narrative Production. Norwood, NJ: Ablex, 1980.

Tapscott, Don. Growing Up Digital: The Rise of the Net Generation. New York: McGraw-Hill, 1998. *The author profiles the rise of the Net Generation, which is using digital technology to change the way individuals and society interact. He makes a distinction between the passive medium of television and the "explosion" of interactive digital media, sparked by the computer and the Internet.*

Thomas, Rosalind. Oral Tradition and Written Record in Classical Athens. Cambridge: Cambridge University Press, 1989. *A leading researcher explores the relationships of orality and literacy in the first major interaction of the two, in classical Athens. As with many similar historical studies, this one helps the reader understand what preceded literacy and also provides a basis for trying to project what could happen when literacy is introduced into a previously-oral culture.*

Thomas, Rosalind. Literacy and Orality in Ancient Greece. Cambridge: Cambridge University Press, 1992. *Thomas extends her research beyond Athens to include ancient Greece as a whole.*

UNESCO. Functional Literacy: Why and How. Paris: UNESCO, 1971.

UNESCO. Practical Guide to Functional Literacy. Paris: UNESCO, 1973.

*Van Rheenen, Gailyn. Communicating Christ in Animistic Contexts. Grand Rapids: Baker Book House, 1991. *This is an excellent book about the communication task of the missionary evangelist when facing an animistic worldview. While based on the author's study in Kenya among the Kipsigis people, the book broadly approaches animism in today's world, the process of theological thinking in animistic contexts and then analyzes animistic practices and powers. It concludes with a comparison of sin and salvation in Christianity and animism. One of the best overall texts on looking at spiritual worldviews and how they relate to communication of the gospel.*

Van Vleck, Amelia B. Memory and Re-Creation in Troubadour Lyric. Berkeley, CA: University of California Press, 1991.

Vansina, Oral Tradition: A Study of Historical Methodology. London: Routledge and Kegan Paul, 1961. *Translated from the original in French, this is a somewhat technical treatise on oral tradition as verbal testimony. The chapter on historical knowledge is of interest to the narrative oral storyteller.*

*Walsh, John. The Art of Storytelling. Chicago: Moody Press, 2003. *This book is a practical guide to storytelling written by a storyteller who overcame his stuttering and fear to tell stories professionally. Walsh includes fine learning activities to use alone or with others. He discusses the use of stories both inside church and out.*

*Weber, Hans Rudi. The Communication of the Gospel to Illiterates. London: SCM, 1957. *This is a case study from Weber's missionary experience among the Luwuk-Banggai people of the Celebes (Indonesia)* *in 1952. Weber looks at the world of illiterates and how they communicate their ideas. He then proposes using oral and visual means of presenting a holistic historical Bible message. While not a treatise about the use of chronological biblical narratives per se, the book contains many fundamental principles for communicating the gospel to illiterates.*

Willmington, H. L <u>Willmington's Guide to the Bible</u>. Carol Stream, IL: Tyndale House Publishers, 1981. *A one-volume guide to the Bible in which the Bible story is first presented chronologically. This is followed by a section called "The Theological Method" in which the major doctrines are presented including the doctrines of the Trinity, the Father, the Son, the Spirit, man, the Church, salvation, Satan, angels, the Bible, and prophecy. The last sections include Topical and Historical Study Summaries.*

*Wright, N. T. <u>The New Testament and the People of God</u>. Minneapolis: Fortress Press, 1992. *This book is a rich and penetrating historical and theological spotlight on first-century Palestinian Judaism, delving into the history, social make-up, worldview, beliefs, and hope of it. One fascinating aspect of the book is how Wright explores worldview and the effect stories have on the shaping of worldview.*

Yates, Francis. <u>The Art of Memory.</u> London: Routledge and Kegan Paul; Chicago: University of Chicago Press, 1966.

Articles

Gilbert Ansre, "The Crucial Role of Oral-Scripture: Focus Africa" in <u>International Journal of Frontier Missions</u> 12 (Apr.-June 1995), 65-68. *Ansre argues that providing Scripture in audio recordings is crucial in reaching both illiterate and post-literate Africans with the gospel.*

Kenneth Bailey, "Informal, Controlled, Oral Tradition and the Synoptic Gospels" in <u>Asia Journal of Theology</u> 5 (1991), 34-54. *Written by an expert on Middle Eastern peasant society, this is a little-known but crucial study showing that there are distinctly different patterns for oral transmission within a Middle Eastern peasant society. Bailey contends that peasants in upper Egypt carefully transmit valued stories without change while allowing alterations to stories of other kinds. They clearly keep the various kinds of stories separate and transmit them using different guidelines.*

Jim Bowman, "Communicating Christ through Oral Tradition: A Training Model for Grass Roots Church Planters" in International Journal of Frontier Missions 20 (Spring 2003), 25-27. *Bowman describes his pilgrimage into training grass roots church planters using oral means.*

Rick Brown, "Communicating God's Message in Oral Cultures" in International Journal of Frontier Missions 21 (Fall 2004), 26-32. *Brown describes oral cultures in contrast with print cultures and suggests principles and strategies for communicating effectively within oral cultures. He discusses choosing Scripture passages, sequencing them, and determining which medium of communication to use.*

Rick Brown. "Selecting and Using Scripture Portions Effectively in Frontier Missions," in International Journal of Frontier Missions 18 (Winter 2001), 10-24. *Brown does an excellent job of describing the criteria for selecting biblical stories in working with oral peoples and why sequencing stories chronologically is so effective.*

Paul D. Dyer, "Was Jesus a Zairian?" in International Journal of Frontier Missions 12 (Apr.-June 1995), 83-86. *Dyer argues that using the heart language on tape makes "Jesus talk" meaningful and receptor oriented. It is received with positive response and greater receptivity to the gospel.*

Hans Magnus Enzensberger, "In Praise of Illiteracy" in Harper's 273 (October 1986), 12-14. *Enzensberger tracks the beginning of the term "illiteracy" to 1876 and notes that the use of the concept is linked to the spread of colonialism.*

Jack Goody, and Ian P. Watt, "The Consequences of Literacy" in Comparative Studies in History and Society 5 (1963), 304-345.

Eric Havelock, "*Dikaiosune:* An Essay in Greek Intellectual History," in Phoenix 23 (1969), 49-70.

Herbert V. Klem, "Dependence on Literacy Strategy: Taking a Hard Second Look" in International Journal of Frontier Missions 12 (Apr.-June 1995), 59-64.

Jean M. Mandler, Sylvia Scribner, Michael Cole, and Marsha DeForest, "Cross-cultural Invariance in Story Recall" in Child Development 51 (1980), 19-26. *This article looks at the childhood development of cognitive schemata and the process of schematic activation.*

S. Devasahayam Ponraj, and Chandan K. Sah, "Communication Bridges to Oral Cultures: A Method that Caused a Breakthrough in Starting Several church planting movements in North India" in International Journal of Frontier Missions 20 (Spring 2003), 28-31.

Sylvia Scribner and Michael Cole, "Cognitive Consequences of Formal and Informal Education," in Science 9 (November 1973), 553-559. *The authors discuss the different goals of formal (literate) and informal (non-literate) education, noting that non-literate children are sometimes labeled as cognitively deficient when no true deficiency exists.*

Viggo Søgaard, "The Emergence of Audio-Scriptures in Church and Mission" in International Journal of Frontier Missions 12 (Apr.-June 1995), 71-75. *A long-time advocate of the use of audio cassettes in Christian ministry explains why that is important and how it is having an impact.*

Tom A. Steffen, "Storying the Storybook to Tribals: A Philippines Perspective of the Chronological Teaching Model," in International Journal of Frontier Missions 12 (Apr.-June 1995), 99-105. *Steffen reports on a survey he did to evaluate the effectiveness of the Chronological Teaching method, developed by Trevor McIlwain and used by many groups.*

Paul C. Vitz, "The Use of Stories in Moral Development: New Psychological Reasons for an Old Education Method," in American Psychologist 45 (June 1990), 709-720. *Contemporary approaches to moral development and moral education emphasize propositional thinking and verbal discussion of abstract moral dilemmas. In contrast, this article proposes that narratives (stories) are a central factor in a person's moral development. Vitz proposes that narratives and narrative thinking are especially involved in how these processes lead to moral development and therefore that narrative should be rehabilitated as a valuable part of moral education. He includes an extensive bibliography from his discipline.*

Dissertations and Theses

Box, Harry. "Communicating Christianity to Oral, Event-Oriented People." D. Miss., Fuller Theological Seminary, Pasadena, CA, 1992.

Dyer, Paul D. "The Use of Oral Communication Methods (Storytelling, Song/Music, and Drama) in Health Education, Evangelism, and Christian Maturation." D. Min., Bethel Seminary, St. Paul, MN, 1994.

Wilson, John D. "Scripture in an Oral Culture: The Yali of Irian Jaya." Th.M., Faculty of Divinity, University of Edinburgh, Edinburgh, 1988.

▷ glossary
for making disciples
of oral learners

○

THESE terms and definitions have been gathered from a variety of sources. This is not an exhaustive list and the definitions are not necessarily universally agreed upon. This is a work in progress. Some definitions will be revised after knowledgeable people continue to make suggestions. The terms below are part of the larger discussion about "making disciples of oral learners."

aliteracy A lack of interest in or enjoyment of reading; characteristic of people who are capable of reading with understanding but do not often read for pleasure. See 'post-literate'.

barriers The aspects of a culture, circumstances, or religion that hinder a listener in hearing, understanding, or acting upon the message of the Gospel. These are the 'stumbling blocks'. Barriers are discerned by studying the worldview. Barriers are beliefs, practices, or experiences that might keep unbelievers from understanding or accepting spiritual truths. Prior experiences, such as with nominal Christians, may also pose barriers. See 'bridges'.

basic Bible truths Those biblical truths which are the foundation or essence of truth leading to salvation, the New Testament Church, the discipled life and Christian leadership. The actual body of truths as expressed may vary somewhat for each worldview situation according to prior knowledge and belief. The three terms 'essential Bible Truths', 'Basic Bible Truths' and 'Universal Bible Truths' all describe the generic or basic truths needed for one of the core objectives such as evangelism, congregationalizing a people (or planting a church), discipling, leader training, etc. See 'essential Bible truths', 'universal Bible truths'.

Bible panorama A selection of stories from the Old and New Testaments. A panorama gives a relatively fast opportunity to tell the Old Testament stories, which provide background and a foundation, as well as the New Testament stories. Alternate term for 'mini Bible' or 'panoramic Bible'. See 'fast-tracking', 'mini Bible, 'panoramic Bible'.

Bible storying A generic term which includes the many forms of telling Bible stories, of which Chronological Bible Storying is the main format. Single stories related to ministry needs, thematic story clusters in teaching and preaching, and even storying which begins with the story of Jesus are sometimes used, according to need and strategy.

Bibleless people group A language group or ethnic group which does not yet possess a translation of the Bible, especially the New Testament scriptures.

bridges The beliefs, practices, or experiences of a culture that can have a beneficial influence upon a person's consideration of the gospel. God-given opportunities for witness, in which needs felt within the culture are met by the Christian faith. Bridges are discerned by studying the 'worldview'. Bridges often provide openings for heightened interest and greater relevancy of the biblical message to a person's worldview. The storyer can intentionally target issues deemed significant to the listener.

CBS See 'Chronological Bible Storying' (acronym)

chirographic Pertaining to a writing culture.

chronological Arranged in the order that things happened in time.

Chronological Bible Storying (CBS) A method of sharing biblical truths by telling the stories of the Bible as intact stories in the order that they happened in time. The person using this method leads the hearers to discover the truths in the stories for the purpose of evangelization, discipleship, church planting, and leader training. Jim Slack and J. O. Terry developed CBS when they saw the need for a purely oral approach to oral peoples. They coined the term 'storying' to differentiate CBS from Chronological Bible Teaching (see below). CBS is promoted globally by the IMB (the International Mission Board of the Southern Baptist Convention).

Chronological Bible Storytelling The act of presenting biblical truth generally in story format though the story may be deeply paraphrased or may be interrupted for teaching whenever some important issue occurs in the passage. The story may or may not be kept intact as a story. It follows a chronologically organized timeline.

Chronological Bible Teaching The type of chronological Bible instruction used by New Tribes Mission, popularized by Trevor McIlwain in the 1970s. It references biblical stories but does not necessarily tell them as intact stories. It uses exposition and explanation as teaching approaches. This presupposes at least semi-literacy on the part of the teacher. CBT methodology reflects NTM's mission of literacy development in conjunction with translation, evangelism, and church planting. See 'New Tribes Mission' and http://www.ntm.org.

church planting movement A rapidly-multiplying increase of indigenous churches planting churches with a given people group or population segment. A church planting movement is not simply an increase in the number of churches, even though this also is positive. A church planting movement occurs when the vision of churches planting churches spreads from the missionary and professional church planter into the churches themselves, so that by their very nature they are winning the lost and reproducing themselves.

communication The process of giving and understanding a message.

communication preference The preferred style or method of communication for an individual or group of people. There are two dominant poles in a communication preference continuum—oral and literate. There are major differences between literate or print-oriented communicators and oral communicators in the way they receive information. See 'literate communicator' and 'oral communicator'.

context ...the whole cognitive environment of the speaker and addressee: their worldview(s), their culture(s), the situation in which they are communicating, their conventions of communication, the immediate context of what they have already said, and any other shared information.

core story, core story list Core stories are those biblical stories which are so essential to the biblical message and/or so consistently relevant in a variety of cultures that they have been chosen again and again as missionaries put together worldview-specific story sets. A core story list, then, is descriptive rather than prescriptive; it acknowledges the stories that have been used most often in evangelism story sets. It is not intended as a 'universal' list that must always be used, but rather it provides an opportunity to see what other storyers have done. (Initially, the core story list reflected the basic list of stories which included and taught the basic truths leading to evangelism, church planting, discipling, or leader training. The most popular list is that for evangelism.) See 'training story set'.

crafting a story, story crafting Crafting Bible stories is shaping the stories from a literature format to an oral format and making such changes as needed to maintain a clear focus on the story's main point(s), to give clarity in telling, and to make necessary changes needed for accommodating certain worldview issues and story continuity leading to the storying track objective of evangelism, discipling, leader training, etc. "Crafting Bible Stories for Telling", an unpublished booklet by J. O. Terry, is available in e-format from: biblestorying@sbcglobal.net

discovery question A question that leads the people to draw a conclusion and discover a biblical truth based on events that occur in a story. Compare 'factual question'.

discovery time The period after the story when the storyer fixes the story in the people's minds by asking someone from the group to retell the story. The storyer then leads the people to discover biblical truths by asking questions about the story.

door opener A kind of 'bridge' involving differences which appeal to the audience. Door openers appeal to people and encourage them to open their hearts and minds to hear the message. For example, Joseph forgave his brothers; this is a new value to people who emphasize honor through vengeance. They are also impressed that God was working in Joseph's life to bring good out of the bad things his brothers did; this is a new concept of God for some people. This appeals to them and opens the door to hear more of the Word. See 'bridges'.

embedded truth Truth that is embedded, retained, situated in, related to, the story and which is evident to the listener without the need to extract the truth in order for the listeners to be aware of its presence and to catch its implication for them. See 'extracted truth'.

engagement/engaged A people group is engaged when a church planting strategy, consistent with evangelical faith and practice, is under implementation. (In this respect, a people group is not engaged when it has been merely adopted, is the object of focused prayer, or is part of an advocacy strategy.)

essential Bible truths Biblical concepts or teachings that are applicable to all Christians, in all cultures. The biblical 'givens' that must be communicated in ministry because without them Christianity loses its distinctiveness. Sometimes referred to as biblical principles. See 'basic Bible truths', 'universal Bible truths', 'core story'.

ethnography A description of a culture. A description of the behavior and lifestyle of a people—a community, society, or ethnic group. The aim in ethnography is to understand another way of life from the 'insider's' point of view. Rather than studying people, ethnography means learning from people. An enquiry into the culture, life, and lifestyles of a specific ethnolinguistic people group. A traditional term for 'worldview'.

evangelical An evangelical Christian is a person who believes that Jesus Christ is the sole source of salvation through faith in Him, has personal faith and conversion with regeneration by the Holy Spirit, recognizes the inspired word of God as the only basis for faith and Christian living, and is committed to biblical preaching and evangelism that brings others to faith in Jesus Christ. Therefore, an evangelical church is a church that is characterized by these same beliefs and principles. Some churches that are not considered evangelical in faith and practice may contain members who are evangelical.

evangelism track   The first set of stories, taught for the purpose of sharing the gospel with unbelievers or giving believers a firm foundation in God's Word.

extracted truth   Truth that is extracted, that is, drawn out of a story and presented as a list of facts, issues, propositions which comprise the essence of the story. Compare 'embedded truth'.

factual question   A question that can be answered from events that happened in the story without much, if any, interpretive insight. Deals with who, what, when, and where. Compare 'discovery question'.

fast-tracking The act of telling many biblical stories one after another at a single occasion with little or no opportunity given for discussion of the stories. Used to give a panorama of the biblical story, to test for receptivity, and to give witness when there is a limited window for contact, among other reasons. Formerly called 'mainstreaming'. See 'Bible panorama'.

functional illiterate / (functional illiteracy)   UNESCO has recommended the following definition: "A person is functionally illiterate who cannot engage in all those activities in which literacy is required for effective functioning of his group and community and also for enabling him to continue to use reading, writing and calculation for his own and the community's development." A person who has had some education but does not meet a minimum standard of literacy. To read poorly and without adequate understanding. Lacks sufficient skills in literacy to function as a literate person in his or her society. Some say that statistics indicate that 70% of the world's population who are either illiterate or functionally illiterate. Please see 'illiterate' for comment on usage.

gaps The difference between potential availability of Scripture and real availability. Language, culture and other barriers and obstacles create a gap between potential and real availability. There are at least four gaps: the translation gap; the distribution gap; the literacy gap; the oral gap. The translation gap includes at least the 2,700 languages with no translation in process and the many languages waiting for Old Testament translation. The distribution gap includes the difference between the number of speakers of languages where a translation has been done and the number of copies of the text which have been printed and distributed. In some major languages there are many more speakers than there are Bibles or New Testaments distributed. The literacy gap exists where a written translated text is available, but speakers of the language are unable to read it. The oral gap exists where there is a translated text, but speakers cannot or will not learn to read it. For such people, audio, video, and radio are possible avenues to access, as well as storytelling.

grass roots evangelism Evangelism at the grassroots level; done by local believers among local believers. Indigenous evangelism resulting in local believers in indigenous churches.

grass roots church planting Church planting at the grassroots level; done by local church planters among local believers using reproducible methodology resulting in indigenous local churches.

Gutenberg Galaxy Term coined by Marshall McLuhan in his book by that name. The time, events and people in history when oral communication styles began to move toward literate communication styles in the West. The 'Gutenberg Galaxy', named for Johannes Gutenberg (renowned as the inventor of printing), is the universe of all printed books ever published. One hypothesis is that a post-Gutenberg universe is emerging based on electronic media.

heart language See 'mother tongue'.

illiterate Not able to read and write. That person is illiterate who, in a language that he speaks, cannot read and understand anything he would have understood if it had been spoken to him; and who cannot write anything that he can say. Note: Because the word 'illiterate' tends to be accompanied by negative connotations, an alternative term to consider using is 'non-literate'. See 'functional' and 'oral preference'.

IMB / International Mission Board of the Southern Baptist Convention. The International Mission Board is an entity of the Southern Baptist Convention, the nation's largest evangelical denomination, which consists of more than 40,000 churches with nearly 16 million members. The IMB's main objective is to present the gospel of Jesus Christ in order to lead individuals to saving faith in Him and resulting in church-planting movements among all the peoples of the world. IMB is one entrance into the Epic Quest program. Specifically, see http://imb.org. More generally, see http://www.sbc.net/.

intact narrative Uninterrupted story which is presented as a whole except for a possible aside or two in the story explaining something unfamiliar to the listeners. Compare 'interrupted narrative' and 'interpreted narrative'.

International Orality Network A network of organizations which are all interested in proclaiming the Scriptures through oral methods. Some members are: Campus Crusade for Christ, DAWN, FCBH, Feba Radio, GRN, IMB, the JESUS Film Project, New Tribes Mission, Scriptures In Use, Trans World Radio, Vernacular Media Services of JAARS, Wycliffe International, and YWAM.

interpreted narrative The story which is explained, or interpreted, without telling the story. It is talking about the story, telling what is in the story, but never telling the story. Compare 'intact narrative' and 'interrupted narrative'.

interrupted narrative Telling the story and stopping, periodically, to teach, emphasizing themes and issues which occur in the story, then continuing the story until another teaching point is reached. Compare 'intact narrative' and 'interpreted narrative'.

key terms / key biblical terms A set of basic biblical vocabulary which includes the words for 'God', 'sin', 'punishment', 'sacrifice', 'reconciliation', 'promise', 'Savior' and more. There are not words for these biblical terms in all languages, or there may be words in some languages which could be used but which might carry meanings which will not accurately convey the biblical sense. Determining key terms is an important component of Bible translation.

learning preference A learning preference is the most common, comfortable and natural way that an individual receives and communicates information. Literate and oral are the two learning preferences discussed in relation to storying. Compare 'communication preference'.

linking Linking provides connectedness between stories. Carefully spanning time (spacers) and generations (place markers) so that the people know that events happened, but do not have the full details, so that the emotional investment in characters is not lost and the storyer can return to that spot in the future and provide additional stories to fill out the biblical chronology.

listening task A fact or truth that the storyer asks the people to listen for in a story.

literate That person is literate who, in a language that he speaks, can read and understand anything he would have understood if it had been spoken to him; and who can write, so that it can be read, anything that he can say.

literate communicator One whose preferred or most effective communication or learning method is in accordance with literate formats. Literate format or style expresses itself through analytic, sequential, linear, and logical thought patterns. Most missionaries are literate communicators, trying to reach oral communicators. See 'oral communicator'.

Lives of the Prophets and Lives of the Apostles A series of booklets prepared for use in the '10/40 Window' consisting of translated biblical passages which present stories of biblical characters and introduce biblical themes. These have been dramatized for audio media and radio broadcast as well.

Lomé 'Y' The Y-shaped diagram which depicts the planning process by which a storyer selects and prepares a set of stories for use in ministry, while keeping in mind the dual concerns of faithfulness to the Bible and meaningfulness to the specific worldview. Named after the place where this was first developed: Lomé, Togo. See 'Ten Step Process' for a later planning model.

mainstreaming Storying the Bible without discussion. Used to give an overview or when presentation time is limited. The storyer simply goes from story to story with appropriate linking and bridging comments and stories. More recently this term has been replaced by 'fast-tracking' in IMB usage. See 'fast-tracking'.

mini-Bible A selection of portions from the Old and New Testaments chosen to fit the context and needs of the receptor-language community. Analogous to 'story set' or 'storying track' and 'Bible panorama' or 'panoramic Bible'.

mother tongue A person's first language; the language of the hearth and home; a person's heart language; the language a person understands best; the language of fear, grief, joy, love, devotion and intimacy; the cherished language learned in infancy between mother and child.

multi-media 'Multi-media' more commonly refers to a combination of text, graphics, pictures, sound, etc. See 'aliteracy', 'post-literate' and 'secondary oral communicators'.

New Tribes Mission NTM is a missionary organization that plants churches in tribal communities to reach people who have never had opportunity to hear the gospel. NTM employs a method of Bible instruction called 'Chronological Bible Teaching'. See www.ntm.org.

non-literate An alternative term for 'illiterate'. See 'illiterate'.

non-print media Audio and videocassette tapes, disks, film, VCD, DVD, etc. Communications media other than print.

OneStory A partnership managed by Campus Crusade, IMB, Trans World Radio, Wycliffe and YWAM. The aim of this partnership is to provide new strategies and resources that will enable the Church to use Chronological Bible Storying as a primary means of reaching the remaining unreached people groups of the world. The vision of OneStory is to help reach the remaining unreached people groups with the gospel in the way that best communicates to them. For most, this will require an oral approach. "The ultimate goal is to provide the entire counsel of God in the heart language of every person in a distribution format accessible to all" (from Epic Vision and Priorities document.) An initial outcome of the partnering effort is a three part introductory set of chronological Bible stories, forty to fifty stories, aimed at supporting initial indigenous-led and reproducing churches. There is no standard story set being promoted. Rather the particular set of stories varies for each people group — a redemptive panorama selected and crafted to best interact with the worldview of each group. This includes stories from the Old Testament, the Gospels, and Acts and the Epistles. See http://www.OneStory.org.

OneStory Quest A two-year internship program specifically devoted to Bible storying for an unreached people group. Entrance to OneStory Quest is through Campus Crusade, IMB (including the Journeyman/ISC program), Wycliffe Bible Translators, or YWAM. An OneStory program.

OneStory Venture Cooperative project of one year or less in which some short-term helpers come alongside a team in a long-term assignment specifically to further the chronological Bible storying approach. An OneStory program.

oral Bible There is no definitive oral Bible. The working definition of oral Bible is: 'The accumulated Bible stories that have been told to an oral society.' Typically, this is between 50 and 225 stories. These are usually told in chronological order, though not always, since many times specific problems, concerns, fears etc. may need to be addressed first. So an oral Bible may differ to some extent from one culture to another, depending on felt and/or actual needs, worldview, theology and so forth. Those stories which form the cornerstone of Christian faith will be represented in virtually all oral Bible collections. An oral Bible is the accumulated Bible stories that have been storied to an oral communicator or that can be recalled by memory. "For many oral communicators the only Bible they will have and effectively use is the one they have in their heads and hearts. It is this Bible, an 'oral Bible', that enables them to meditate upon God's Word in their quiet times and devotionals and use it in evangelism, discipleship, church planting, and leadership development. This oral Bible can go where many times the written Bible cannot go. It can cross borders, enter prisons... An oral Bible becomes the permanent possession of an oral communicator and is available for use at all times. Oral communicators are able to retain, recall, and repeat from memory their oral Bible."

oral communicator Someone who prefers to learn or process information by oral rather than written means. (Thus, there are literate people whose preferred communication style is oral rather than literate, even though they can read.) Also, someone who cannot read or write. Someone whose preferred or most effective communication and learning format, style, or method is in accordance with oral formats, as contrasted to literate formats.

oral preference A preference for receiving and processing information in an oral format rather than print. That person may or may not be a reader. See 'oral communicator'.

orality Almost two-thirds of the world's population is illiterate (non-literate, preliterate) or has an oral preference (can't, won't or don't read and write.) The quality or state of being oral. The constellation of characteristics (cognitive, communicational, and relational) that are typical of cultures that function orally. See http://www. chronologicalbiblestorying.com/MANUAL/section x.htm for "109 Characteristics of Oral and Literate Communicators".

oral story models Sets of stories which are determined and agreed upon during a training session and later used by those being trained without having been written down. The outcome, primarily, of story training sessions with oral leaders. Stories are selected through study and suggestion of the trainer and the intuition of those being trained. Critical teaching truths and issues related to understanding and acceptance of the stories is discussed during the training.

oral tradition Oral traditions are unwritten sources couched in a form suitable for oral transmission. Their preservation depends upon the powers of memory of successive generations of human beings. Oral traditions consist of verbal testimonies which are repeatedly-reported statements, either spoken or sung, concerning the past. Oral tradition is a memory of memories in the most literal way, since the message is learned from what another person recalled and told. "Whenever an African bushman dies, a whole [oral] library goes out of existence." See http://www.chronologicalbiblestorying.com/MANUAL/section x.htm for "109 Characteristics of Oral and Literate Communicators".

panoramic Bible   Alternate term for 'mini Bible' or 'Bible panorama'.

people group A significantly large grouping of individuals who perceive themselves to have a common affinity for one another because of their shared language, religion, ethnicity, residence, occupation, class or caste, situation, etc. or combinations of these. For evangelistic purposes: The largest group within which the gospel can spread as a church-planting movement without encountering barriers of understanding or acceptance.

phase There are phases in the church-planting and evangelism effort, for example, a Church Planting Phase and a Church Strengthening Phase. In CBS, 'storying tracks' are utilized within phases. Within the Church Planting phase there are typically five tracks: Evangelism, Discipleship, Church Planting, Characterization, and The End Times.

Within the Church Strengthening Phase there are an indefinite number of tracks, addressing maturing believers, corrective and instructive themes, church leader training, and other topics, like preaching tracks. See 'story set' and 'storying track'.

point-of-ministry storying See 'situational storying'.

post-literate At the close of the 20th century, the phenomenon in which even those who can read and write well are not doing so. The epoch of the audio-visual, termed by some 'the Multi-Media Era', has set in. Some writers also use the term 'aliteracy' to describe this phenomenon. See 'aliteracy', 'multi media,' and 'secondary oral communicators'.

post-story dialog The teaching/learning time following the told Bible story when a story is retold by listeners, listening tasks are reviewed, or discovery questions and comments are made to draw out and relate story truths to listeners' lives.

pre-evangelism The process of preparing unbelievers to hear the gospel. This involves choosing a location to hold the storying sessions, building relationships and investigating the people's worldview. This may include the telling of a few topical Bible stories to generate interest in the audience for the evangelism set of stories, such as water stories told during a well drilling project, or grief stories for the bereaved, etc.

pre-story dialog A time before the Bible story is told when proper cultural greeting, review of previous stories, needed background stories or information, and sensitizing questions or comments are made to prepare listeners for the following Bible story.

primary oral culture Cultures with no knowledge at all of writing

primary orality The state of persons totally unfamiliar with writing. People who have never 'seen' a word.

receptor language In translation, this is the language one is translating into, not from. Opposite of source language. 'Receptor' is similar to 'target'.

reproduce, reproducing, reproducible A Christian, an indigenous church, and/or a strategy of evangelism and church planting able to multiply or affect multiplication without outside help.

Self-replicating, as in 'self-supporting, self-governing, and self-replicating.'

residual orality This describes those who have been exposed to literacy, even learned to read in school, but who retain a strong preference for learning by oral rather than literate means.

rhetoric The art of speaking or writing effectively. Specifically, the study of principles and rules of composition formulated by critics of ancient times. Also, the skill of the effective use of speech.

Scripture In Use or Scripture Use See SIU or SU below.

Scriptures In Use The name of an organization which specializes in training indigenous church planters in methods of Bible storytelling and other oral communications methods. See http://www.siutraining.org. In addition, please see SIU or SU below.

secondary oral communicators People who depend on electronic audio and visual communications (multimedia). It is said that in some developing countries people are moving directly from primary orality to secondary orality without passing through an orientation to print. "So as nonprint media become available to them, they move from being primary oral societies to becoming multimedia societies, skipping the stage of literacy." See 'aliteracy', 'post-literate'.

semi-literate Able to read and write on an elementary level, especially when working with familiar documents and familiar ideas. Able to read but poor in communicating through writing. Students in 10th grade are often characterized as semi-literate, especially if the quality of their schooling is inadequate. If the educational system utilizes rote memory as the dominant approach to learning, even high school graduates may test out at semi-literate functionality. This is also true of some high school graduates who spend their final years in a vocational/technical training curriculum instead of a more academic, college preparatory curriculum.

session See 'story session'.

shell story models Those model story sets which outline the basic considerations for storying to a given people group and their typical worldview with its barriers and bridges to the gospel. A list of recommended Bible stories and teaching themes are given which relate to the worldview and foundational truths of the gospel the people need to hear. The stories are not fleshed out in their entirety but are given only in a listing or outline with a scripture reference base and possibly a list of the teaching points. The user must complete or fill up the shell in his preparation of the stories in the language to be used in storying.

SIL SIL International is a faith-based organization that studies, documents and assists in developing the world's lesser-known languages. Its staff shares a Christian commitment to service, academic excellence, and professional engagement through literacy, linguistics, translation, and other disciplines. One aim of SIL is to provide access to the Scriptures in the language and format (media) that best serves the people. SIL is an organization related to Wycliffe. See http://www.sil.org.

situational storying or point-of-ministry storying The use of appropriate Bible stories (often those of Jesus' ministry) during a ministry need or opportunity. The primary reason is to lift up Jesus, followed by an invitation to hear more stories. Other story themes may be used appropriate to the ministry activity, such as The Water Stories or The Hope Stories, for disaster relief and ministry.

SIU or SU Acronym for 'Scripture in Use'. Generally, 'Scripture in use' or 'Scripture use' refers to varied methods to get the translated Scriptures into use in people's lives other than literacy. These other methods include audio and videocassette recordings, indigenous music, Scripture-in-song and Bible Storying. (SIL has a Scripture Use Coordinator on a par with the Linguistic, Literacy, and Translation Coordinators.) In addition, please see 'Scripture In Use' above. (Note: SU is also the acronym for 'Scripture Union'.)

source / source language In translation, this is the language one is translating from, not into (for example, New Testament Greek.) Opposite of receptor or target language.

story crafting See 'crafting'.

story session/storying session/session The actual time when the storyer uses the storying method. During a session the storyer participates in opening conversation, reads from the Bible, tells the story, and leads discovery (dialog) time.

story set   A collection of biblical stories selected for a specific ministry purpose and usually arranged in chronological order. In an initial CBS strategy, this typically consists of an evangelism story set, discipleship story set, and church-planting story set. The evangelism story set normally contains a series of stories from the Old Testament and the gospels. Church planting story sets draw from the book of Acts. Many evangelism story sets have included 20 to 25 stories that are common to most story sets; this is considered a starting point for adding other stories that present 'bridges' and address 'barriers' specific to the worldview of each people group. The first phase sets the foundation for future phases, including evangelism, church planting, discipleship, leadership development, audio-visual products, radio ministry, and Bible translation. The long-range plan is that someone among those participating in the first phase will catch a vision to continue a longer-term work to see the growth of mature churches within that people group. A story set is the list of crafted (or prepared) stories and suggested teaching/ learning activities that compose a track. See 'storying track'.

storyer   The person who uses the storying method to evangelize, disciple or strengthen the church.

storying   The term 'storying' is "an attempt to make a strong statement about the value of the intact, uninterrupted Bible narrative as a valuable means of teaching God's Word leading to salvation, church planting, discipling, leader training, and various ministry activities. Storying is not limited in purpose to teaching nonliterates. It is used because it is reproducible by listeners and because the use of story helps to overcome resistance or hostility to traditional Westernized teaching. See 'Chronological Bible Storying' (CBS).

storying matrix   The web or structure of stories that follows the biblical timeline. This is the initial structure given in the first telling of stories or lessons which give an essential biblical framework into which other stories and later truths may be placed.

storying scarf   The Storying Scarf is a cotton scarf designed to put an inexpensive set of durable pictures representing God's Word in the hands of people who could use it to independently share God's word where missionaries cannot go. It is designed to be used in conjunction with a series of 21 chronologically-arranged Bible stories. See http://storyingscarf.com.

storying track The entire series of stories typically arranged in chronological order which have been selected for presentation to a target population for the purpose of evangelism, discipleship or leadership training, whichever the case may be. Some names of tracks are "Evangelism Track", "Review Track", "Last Lessons", or "End Times Track". In CBS, 'storying tracks' are utilized within 'phases'. A 'storying track' is equivalent to a 'story set'. In Chronological Bible Teaching the term 'phase' is used in the same way that 'track' is used to define a set of lessons in CBS. The purpose of the track is to limit the story set to those stories which serve best to accomplish the desired teaching objective. The track is for the benefit of the storyer, but is more or less kept invisible to the listeners. For instance, the storyer does not say, 'Now we will do the Discipleship Track.' See 'story set'.

Table 71 A regular gathering of mission-agency leaders which arose from the Amsterdam 2000 conference. Table 71 has adopted a cooperative strategy centered on orality and Chronological Bible Storying.

target language See 'receptor language'.

target population / target people The group the storyer is seeking to reach. Often an 'unreached people group'. The people that have been selected to whom the storyer will story. See 'receptor'.

Ten Step Process Identifies the preparation needed to develop a Bible story set:

Step One: Identify the biblical principle or truth you want to communicate; make it clear and simple. *Step Two:* Consider the worldview of the chosen people group. *Step Three:* Identify the bridges, barriers, and gaps in their worldview. *Step Four:* Select the appropriate Bible story or stories that will communicate the principle considering the worldview issues of the chosen people. *Step Five:* Craft the story and plan the pre-story and the post-story dialog to emphasize the principle or truth you want to communicate. *Step Six:* Tell the story in a culturally appropriate way, which will be through narrative and perhaps also through song, dance, drama, or other means. *Step Seven:* Facilitate the dialogue with the group to help them discover the meaning and the application without your having to tell them. *Step Eight:* Help the group obey the biblical principle. *Step Nine:* Establish group accountability. *Step Ten:* Encourage the group to reproduce this by modeling the principles in their own life and then telling the stories and discipling other people.

The Seed Company (TSC) An organization devoted to partnering with nationals to plant the seed of God's word; affiliated with Wycliffe. www.theseedcompany.org.

themes Central ideas or truths found in the biblical stories

track / story track A set of stories joined together by specific themes and told for a particular purpose. That list of stories which address a strategy or teaching objective. See 'storying track'.

traditional religion and culture The indigenous religion and culture of a local people.

training story set A redemptive panorama story set that covers the basic elements of a biblical worldview. This consists of the stories found to be common to many storying projects implemented around the world in different contexts in recent years. Compare 'Bible panorama', 'core story list'.

transition story A brief story told to summarize biblical events that happened between the stories in different lessons. Sometimes called a 'linking story'.

turning point Factor which is important in decisions to follow Christ in a target or receptor population.

typographic Of or relating to a print or reading culture.

unengaged See 'engagement'.

universal Bible truths See 'basic Bible truths', core story', 'essential Bible truths'.

unreached people group / UPG More broadly, an ethnic group which does not possess a church and which does not have the presence of an indigenous Christian witness. A people, usually an ethnolinguistic group, with a historical culture, language and often a geographical place of residence where there is little or no presence of evangelical Christianity, especially in the forms of Bible, Christian gospel presentations, believers, baptisms and churches. A people group within which there is no indigenous community of believing

Christians about to evangelize this people group without requiring outside (cross-cultural) assistance. A group is considered 'reached' if it has a viable, indigenous, self-reproducing church movement in its midst. More specifically, a people group in which less than 2% of the population are evangelical Christians.

visual aid A picture, simple drawing, or object that will help the people remember or understand the story. Considerations: Will some pictures confuse or offend listeners due to cultural considerations? Are contextualized pictures helpful? Will the cost limit wider use?

worldview The way a specific people view the world around them. Somewhat like wearing tinted lenses, members of a culture look through their worldview, not at it. A worldview is seldom apparent to its adherents unless it comes under question. A worldview consists of fundamental cognitive, affective, and evaluative assumptions about reality. A worldview forms the core of a culture, which guides people in how to act, think, believe, function, and relate. How people look at life and the world around them, a people's view of the world. A profile of the way people within a specified culture live, act, think, and work and relate.

the context

for the production of the Lausanne Occasional Papers

THE Lausanne Movement is an international movement committed to energising **"the whole Church to take the whole gospel to the whole world"**.

With roots going back to the historical conferences in Edinburgh (1910) and Berlin (1966), the Lausanne Movement was born out of the First International Congress on World Evangelization called by evangelist Billy Graham held in Lausanne, Switzerland, in July 1974. The landmark outcome of this Congress was the ***Lausanne Covenant*** supported by the 2430 participants from 150 nations. The covenant declares the substance of the Christian faith as historically declared in the creeds and adds a clear missional dimension to our faith. Many activities have emerged from the Lausanne Congress and from the second congress held in Manila in 1989. The Covenant (in a number of languages) and details about the many regional events and specialised conferences which have been undertaken in the name of Lausanne may be examined on the website at www.lausanne.org.

The continuing Lausanne International Committee believed it was led by the Holy Spirit to hold another conference which would bring together Christian leaders from around the world. This time the Committee planned to have younger emerging leaders involved and sought funds to enable it to bring a significant contingent from those parts of the world where the church is rapidly growing today. It decided to call the conference a **Forum**. As a Forum its structure would be to allow people to come and participate if they had something to contribute to one of 31 issues. These issues were chosen through a global research programme seeking to identify the most significant issues in the world today which are of concern in our task to take the *good news* to the world.

This Lausanne Occasional Paper (LOP) is the report which has emerged from one of these Issue Groups. LOPs have been produced for each of the Issue Groups and information regarding these and other publications may be obtained by going to the website at www.lausanne.org.

The theme of the Forum for World Evangelization held in 2004 was **"A new vision, a new heart and a renewed call"**. This Forum was held in Pattaya, Thailand from September 29 to October 5, 2004. 1530 participants came from 130 countries to work in one of the 31 Issue Groups.

The Affirmations at the conclusion of the Forum stated:
There has been a spirit of working together in serious dialogue and prayerful reflection. Representatives from a wide spectrum of cultures and virtually all parts of the world have come together to learn from one another and to seek new direction from the Holy Spirit for world evangelization. They committed themselves to joint action under divine guidance.

The dramatic change in the political and economic landscape in recent years has raised new challenges in evangelization for the church. The polarization between east and west makes it imperative that the church seek God's direction for the appropriate responses to the present challenges.

In the 31 Issue Groups these new realities were taken into consideration, including the HIV pandemic, terrorism, globalization, the global role of media, poverty, persecution of Christians, fragmented families, political and religious nationalism, post-modern mind set, oppression of children, urbanization, neglect of the disabled and others.

Great progress was made in these groups as they grappled for solutions to the key challenges of world evangelization. As these groups focused on making specific recommendations, larger strategic themes came to the forefront.

There was affirmation that major efforts of the church must be directed toward those who have no access to the gospel. The commitment to help establish self sustaining churches within 6000 remaining unreached people groups remains a central priority.

Secondly, the words of our Lord call us to love our neighbour as ourselves. In this we have failed greatly. We renew our commitment to reach out in love and compassion to those who are marginalised because of disabilities or who have different lifestyles and spiritual perspectives. We commit to reach out to children and young people who constitute a majority of the world's population, many of whom are being abused, forced into slavery, armies and child labour.

A third stream of a strategic nature acknowledges that the growth of the church is now accelerating outside of the western world. Through the participants from Africa, Asia and Latin America, we recognise the dynamic nature and rapid growth of the church in the *South*. Church leaders from the *South* are increasingly providing exemplary leadership in world evangelization.

Fourthly, we acknowledge the reality that much of the world is made up of oral learners who understand best when information comes to them by means of stories. A large proportion of the world's populations are either unable to or unwilling to absorb information through written communications. Therefore, a need exists to share the "Good News" and to disciple new Christians in story form and parables.

Fifthly, we call on the church to use media to effectively engage the culture in ways that draw non believers toward spiritual truth and to proclaim Jesus Christ in culturally relevant ways.

Finally, we affirm the priesthood of all believers and call on the church to equip, encourage and empower women, men and youth to fulfil their calling as witnesses and co-labourers in the world wide task of evangelization.

Transformation was a theme which emerged from the working groups. We acknowledge our own need to be continually transformed, to continue to open ourselves to the leading of the Holy Spirit, to the challenges of God's word and to grow in Christ together with fellow Christians in ways that result in social and economic transformation. We acknowledge that the scope of the gospel and building the Kingdom of God involves, body, mind, soul and spirit. Therefore we call for increasing integration of service to society and proclamation of the gospel.

We pray for those around the world who are being persecuted for their faith and for those who live in constant fear of their lives. We uphold our brothers and sisters who are suffering. We recognize that the reality of the persecuted church needs to be increasingly on the agenda of the whole body of Christ. At the same time, we also acknowledge the importance of loving and doing good to our enemies while we fight for the right of freedom of conscience everywhere.

We are deeply moved by the onslaught of the HIV/AIDS pandemic – the greatest human emergency in history. The Lausanne movement calls all churches everywhere to prayer and holistic response to this plague.

"9/11", the war in Iraq, the war on terror and its reprisals compel us to state that we must not allow the gospel or the Christian faith to be captive to any one geo-political entity. We affirm that the Christian faith is above all political entities.

We are concerned and mourn the death and destruction caused by all conflicts, terrorism and war. We call for Christians to pray for peace, to be proactively involved in reconciliation and avoid all attempts to turn any conflict into a religious war. Christian mission in this context lies in becoming peace makers.

We pray for peace and reconciliation and God's guidance in how to bring about peace through our work of evangelization. We pray for God to work in the affairs of nations to open doors of opportunity for the gospel. We call on the church to mobilize every believer to focus specific consistent prayer for the evangelization of their communities and the world.

In this Forum we have experienced the partnership of men and women working together. We call on the church around the world to work towards full partnership of men and women in the work of world evangelism by maximising the gifts of all.

We also recognize the need for greater intentionality in developing future leaders. We call on the church to find creative ways to release emerging leaders to serve effectively.

Numerous practical recommendations for local churches to consider were offered. These will be available on the Lausanne website and in the Lausanne Occasional Papers. It is our prayer that these many case studies and action plans will be used of God to mobilize the church to share a clear and relevant message using a variety of methods to reach the most neglected or resistant groups so that everyone will have the opportunity to hear the gospel message and be able to respond to this good news in faith.

We express our gratitude to the Thai Church which has hosted us and to their welcoming presentation to the Forum. We are profoundly grateful to God for the privilege of being able to gather here from the four corners of the earth. We have developed new partnerships, made new friends and encouraged one another in our various ministries. Notwithstanding the resistance to the gospel in many places and the richness of an inherited religious and cultural tradition we here at the Forum have accepted afresh the renewed call to be obedient to the mandate of Christ. We commit ourselves to making His saving love known so that the whole world may have opportunity to accept God's gift of salvation through Christ.

These affirmations indicate the response of the participants to the Forum outcomes and their longing that the whole church may be motivated by the outcomes of the Forum to strengthen its determination to be obedient to God's calling.

May the case studies and the practical suggestions in this and the other LOPs be of great help to you and your church as you seek to find new ways and a renewed call to proclaim the saving love of Jesus Christ

David Claydon
Series Editor
2004 Forum LOPs
LCWE

participants
and contributors to this paper

Convener: Avery Willis, USA
Co-convener: Steve Evans, South Asia
Facilitator: Mark Snowden, USA

Victor Anderson . . . . Horn of Africa
Nils Becker . . . . USA
Jim Bowman . . . . USA
Graydon Colville, ... Australia
Steve Douglass . . . . USA
Ron Green . . . . USA
Annette Hall . . . . North Africa
Morgan Jackson . . . . USA
Andrew Kanu . . . . Sierra Leone
Derek Knell . . . . Cyprus
Grant Lovejoy . . . . USA
Durk Meijer . . . . Netherlands
Jay Moon . . . . West Africa
Ted Olsen . . . . USA
David Payne . . . . USA
Roy Peterson . . . . USA
Sheila Ponraj . . . . India
Chandan Sah . . . . India
Dee Douglas . . . . Hungary
David Sills . . . . USA
Jim Slack . . . . USA
Stephen Stringer . . . . West Africa
Tom Tatlow . . . . USA
LaNette Thompson . . . . West Africa
Bob Varney . . . . USA

List of Lausanne Occasional Papers from the 2004 Forum

Issue Group

These papers will be available as a Compendium published by William Carey Library. Online ordering at www.WCLBooks.com Your can download one or more of these LOPs for personal use and see other information on the Lausanne website at www.lausanne.org.